UNDER THE MICROSCOPE

Heart

How the blood gets around the body

Contributors

Author and series consultant: Richard Walker BSc PhD PGCE taught biology, science and health education for several years before becoming a full-time writer. He is a foremost author and consultant specializing in books for adults and children on human biology, health and natural history. He is the author of *Heart: How the blood gets around the body, Making Life: How we reproduce and grow, Muscles: How we move and exercise* and *Brain: Our body's nerve centre* in this series, and is consultant on the whole series.

Advisory panel

1 Heart: How the blood gets around the body
P M Schofield MD FRCP FICA FACC FESC is Consultant Cardiologist at Papworth Hospital, Cambridge

2 Skeleton: Our body's framework
R N Villar MS FRCS is Consultant Orthopaedic Surgeon at Cambridge BUPA Lea Hospital and Addenbrooke's Hospital, Cambridge

3 Digesting: How we fuel the body
J O Hunter FRCP is Director of the Gastroenterology Research Unit, Addenbrooke's Hospital, Cambridge

4 Making Life: How we reproduce and grow
Jane MacDougall MD MRCOG is Consultant Obstetrician and Gynaecologist at the Rosie Maternity Hospital, Addenbrooke's NHS Trust, Cambridge

5 Breathing: How we use air
Mark Slade MA MBBS MRCP is Senior Registrar, Department of Respiratory Medicine, Addenbrooke's Hospital, Cambridge

6 Senses: How we connect with the world
Peter Garrard MA MRCP is Medical Research Council Fellow and Honorary Specialist Registrar, Neurology Department, Addenbrooke's Hospital, Cambridge

7 Muscles: How we move and exercise
Jumbo Jenner MD FRCP is Consultant, and **R T Kavanagh MD MRCP** is Senior Registrar, Department of Rheumatology, Addenbrooke's Hospital, Cambridge

8 Brain: Our body's nerve centre
Peter Garrard MA MRCP is Medical Research Council Fellow and Honorary Specialist Registrar, Neurology Department, Addenbrooke's Hospital, Cambridge

Heart

How the blood gets around the body

Richard Walker

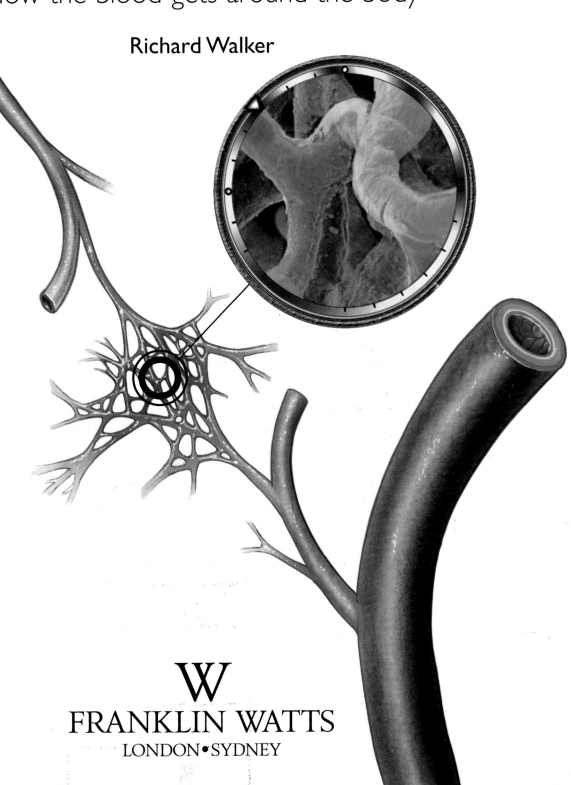

W

FRANKLIN WATTS

LONDON • SYDNEY

ABOUT THIS BOOK

First published in 1998
This edition 2001

Franklin Watts
96 Leonard Street
London EC2A 4XD

Franklin Watts Australia
56 O'Riordan Street
Alexandria
NSW 2015

© Franklin Watts 1998

0 7496 3070 1 (Hardback)
0 7496 4401 X (Paperback)

Dewey Decimal Classification Number: 612.1

A CIP catalogue record for this book is
available from the British Library

Printed in Belgium

Produced for Franklin Watts
by Miles Kelly Publishing
Unit 11
The Bardfield Centre
Great Bardfield
Essex
CM7 4SL

Designed by Full Steam Ahead

Artwork commissioned by
Branka Surla

Illustrated by Roger Stewart

Under the Microscope uses micro-photography to allow you to see right inside the human body.

The camera acts as a microscope, looking at unseen parts of the body and zooming in on the body's cells at work. Some of the micro-photographs are magnified hundreds of times, others thousands of times. They have been dramatically coloured to bring details into crisp focus, and are linked to clear and accurate illustrations that fit them in context inside the body.

New words are explained the first time that they are used, and can also be checked in the glossary at the back of the book.

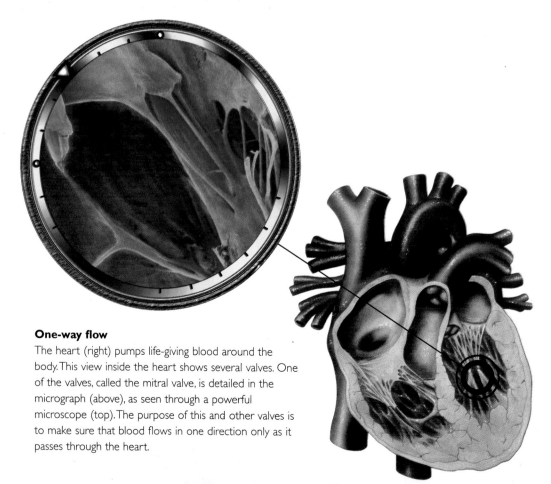

One-way flow
The heart (right) pumps life-giving blood around the body. This view inside the heart shows several valves. One of the valves, called the mitral valve, is detailed in the micrograph (above), as seen through a powerful microscope (top). The purpose of this and other valves is to make sure that blood flows in one direction only as it passes through the heart.

CONTENTS

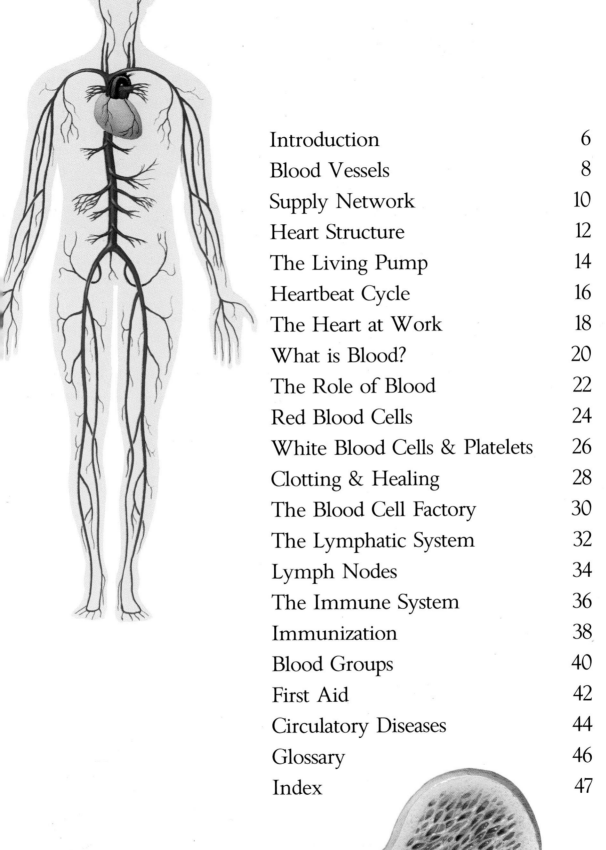

INTRODUCTION

Put one of your hands flat on the middle of your chest. Just a few centimetres below the palm of your hand – under a thin layer of skin, muscle, and bone – is your heart. You might even be able to feel it. It beats non-stop, day and night, all through your life.

The heart is a simple but reliable pump. It pumps blood around the body along tubes called blood vessels. Blood is a red liquid that carries vital food and oxygen to every one of the body's billions of cells, and removes their wastes. Without this minute-by-minute delivery and collection service, all the cells – and the body – would die. That's why the heart has to keep pumping non-stop.

Blood also has an important role in healing wounds and preventing disease. If your skin gets cut and you bleed, the blood automatically seals the opening to halt blood loss. And as blood travels around the body, special cells in the blood watch out for – and deal with – bacteria, viruses and other germs that could make us ill. This volume of **Under the Microscope** zooms in on the heart, blood and blood vessels to explain how they keep our cells alive and defend us from germ attack.

Blood carriers
This special type of X-ray – called an angiogram – shows the main blood vessels that leave the heart. Blood vessels are tubes that carry blood around the body.

Dangerous invaders
The body is constantly under threat from germs, such as this bacterium (left), that can cause diseases. Cells in the blood seek out and destroy invading germs before they can cause any harm. This bacterium (right), called streptococcus, wraps itself in a special coat to hide from the body's defences, making it difficult to get rid of when it infects a person.

Colouring blood
They may look like cushions (right), but these are actually cells, called red blood cells, seen under the microscope. There are billions of red blood cells in a person's blood. They give blood its red colour.

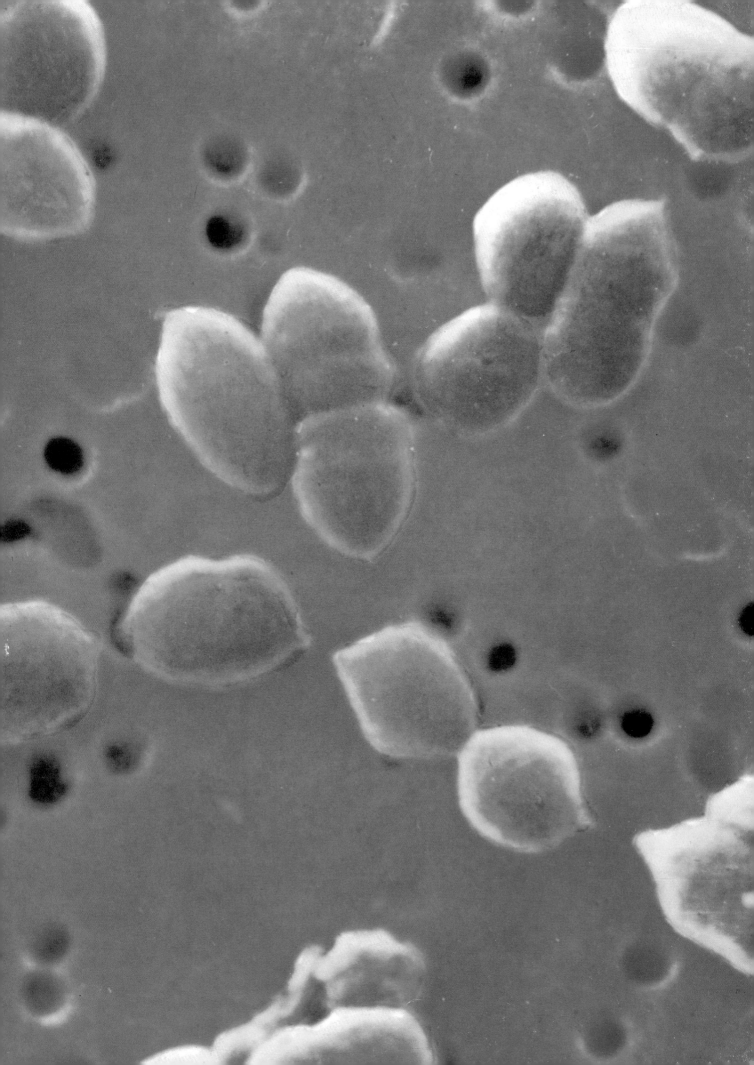

BLOOD VESSELS

A network of tubes called blood vessels extends throughout the body.

Blood vessels carry blood pumped by the heart to all parts of the body, and then transport it back to the heart ready for its next journey. There are three main types of blood vessels in the body: arteries, veins, and capillaries.

Arteries are tough, elastic tubes that carry blood away from the heart, dividing as they do to form smaller and smaller vessels. The largest arteries are as thick as a thumb, while the smallest − called arterioles − are thinner than a hair. Most arteries carry bright red blood that is rich in oxygen.

Veins carry blood towards the heart. The smallest veins − called venules − which, like arterioles, are very thin, join up to form larger and larger veins which eventually open into the heart. Most veins carry dark red blood that is low in oxygen. Linking arteries and veins are the capillaries − the smallest blood vessels.

Heart

Arterial network
This shows the body's main arteries and the parts of the body to which they carry blood.

Arteries
Arteries have thick walls that are both muscular and elastic in order to withstand the high pressure produced when the heart pumps blood along them. Without these thick walls the arteries would burst.

Inside an artery
On the right is a microscopic view of the inside of an artery that carries blood to the leg. The blood carried by these thick-walled vessels contains different types of cells, including these red blood cells.

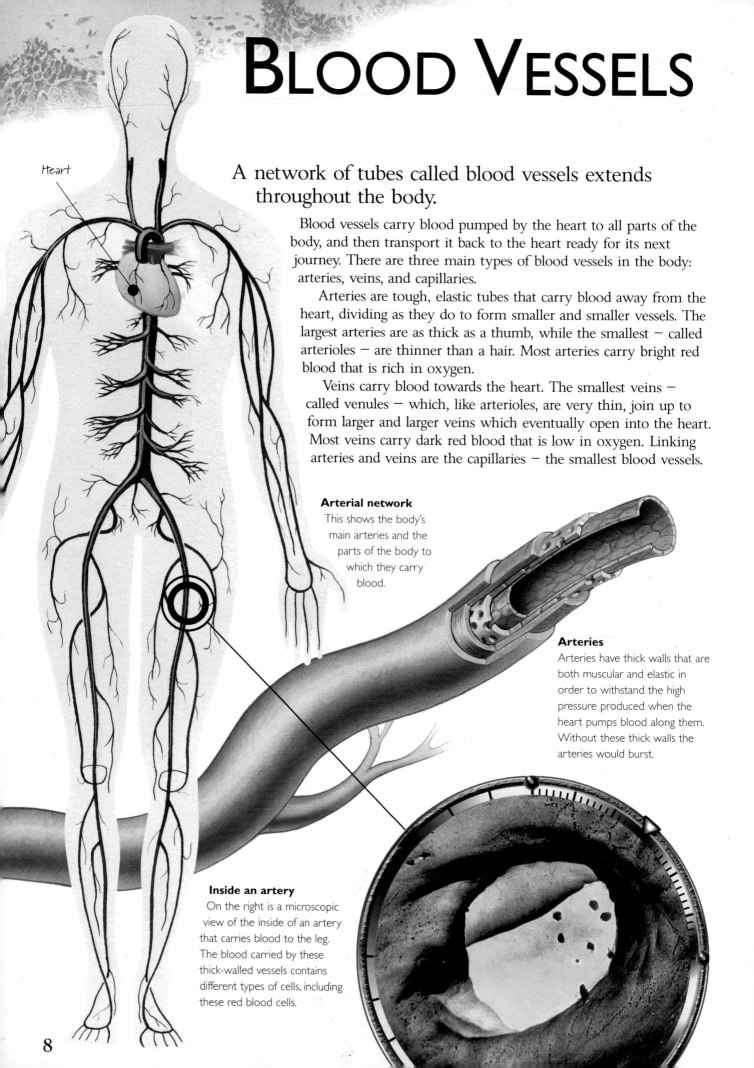

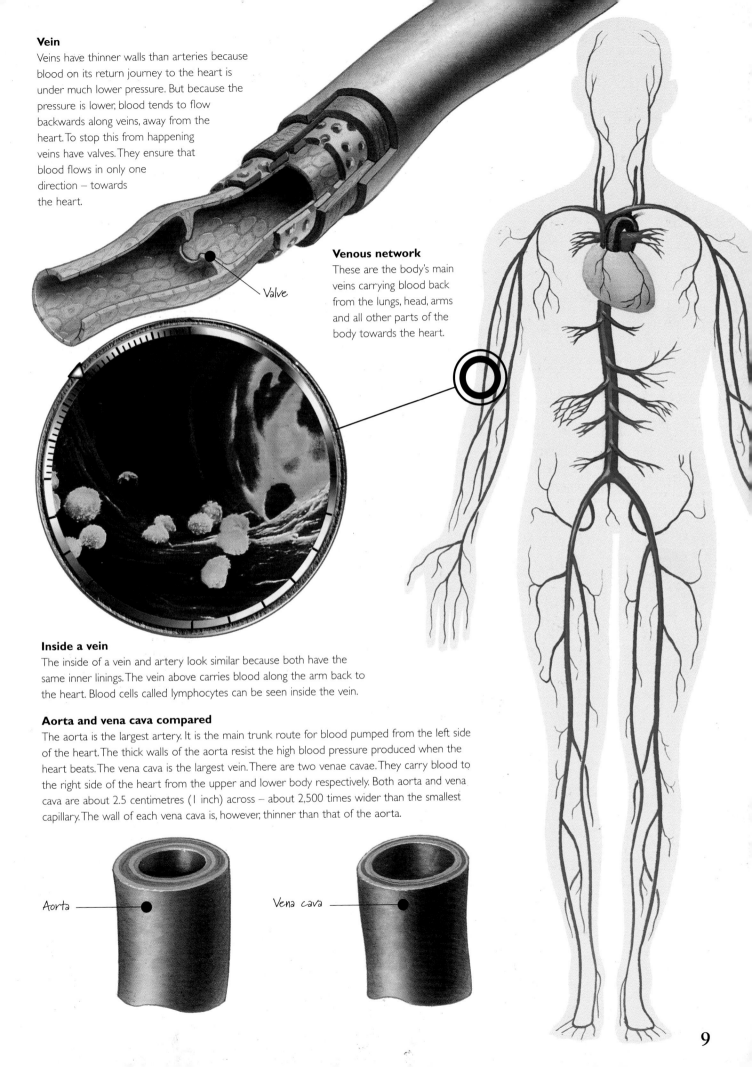

Vein

Veins have thinner walls than arteries because blood on its return journey to the heart is under much lower pressure. But because the pressure is lower, blood tends to flow backwards along veins, away from the heart. To stop this from happening veins have valves. They ensure that blood flows in only one direction – towards the heart.

Valve

Venous network

These are the body's main veins carrying blood back from the lungs, head, arms and all other parts of the body towards the heart.

Inside a vein

The inside of a vein and artery look similar because both have the same inner linings. The vein above carries blood along the arm back to the heart. Blood cells called lymphocytes can be seen inside the vein.

Aorta and vena cava compared

The aorta is the largest artery. It is the main trunk route for blood pumped from the left side of the heart. The thick walls of the aorta resist the high blood pressure produced when the heart beats. The vena cava is the largest vein. There are two venae cavae. They carry blood to the right side of the heart from the upper and lower body respectively. Both aorta and vena cava are about 2.5 centimetres (1 inch) across – about 2,500 times wider than the smallest capillary. The wall of each vena cava is, however, thinner than that of the aorta.

Aorta

Vena cava

SUPPLY NETWORK

The complex network of blood vessels, together with the blood they contain and the heart, make up your circulatory system. It is called a circulatory system because it circulates or moves blood round from the heart to the body's tissues and organs and back to the heart again.

Inside your body the network of blood vessels extends for over 150,000 kilometres (90,000 miles) – over three times the distance round the Earth! Most of the network is made up of the tiny capillaries that pass through the tissues linking arteries to veins. While arteries and veins form the 'highways' and 'main streets' of the circulatory system, the microscopic capillaries are the 'side roads' that deliver to and collect from individual cells.

The circulatory system is really two systems joined together. The pulmonary (lung) circulatory system carries blood from the heart to the lungs where it picks up oxygen, and back to the heart. Notice that in the pulmonary system, unusually, the arteries carry oxygen-poor blood, while the veins carry oxygen-rich blood. The systemic circulatory system serves the rest of the body apart from the lungs. It carries blood to cells in the brain, fingers, stomach, kidneys and all other tissues and organs. Here it delivers oxygen and food and picks up waste.

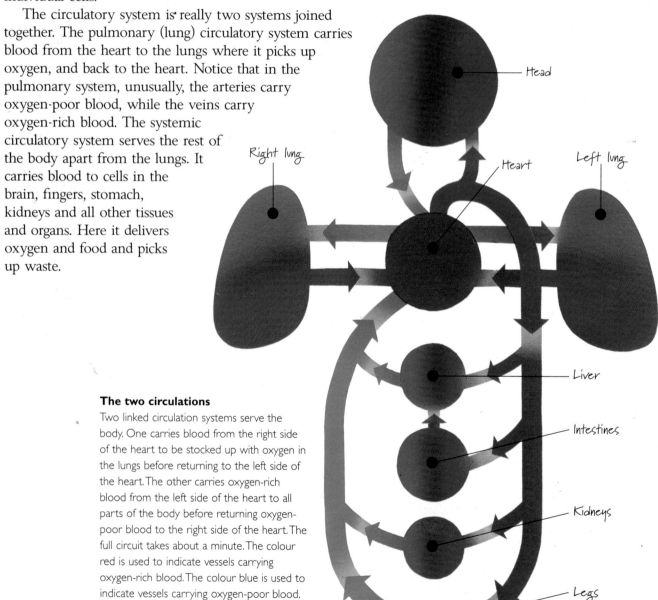

The two circulations
Two linked circulation systems serve the body. One carries blood from the right side of the heart to be stocked up with oxygen in the lungs before returning to the left side of the heart. The other carries oxygen-rich blood from the left side of the heart to all parts of the body before returning oxygen-poor blood to the right side of the heart. The full circuit takes about a minute. The colour red is used to indicate vessels carrying oxygen-rich blood. The colour blue is used to indicate vessels carrying oxygen-poor blood.

Blood capillaries

Seen under the microscope, these tiny tubes twist and turn as they pass through the body's tissues. These branching capillaries are supplying the needs of muscles that move the body. Capillaries are very narrow, and barely wider than the blood cells that they carry.

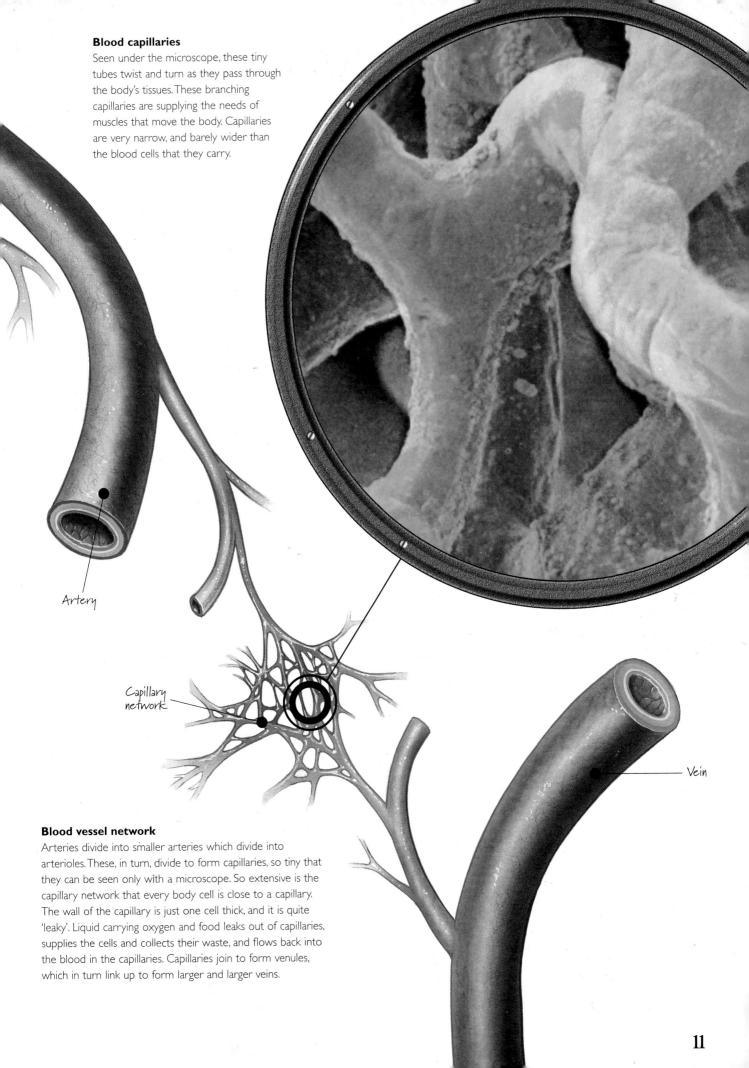

Artery

Capillary network

Vein

Blood vessel network

Arteries divide into smaller arteries which divide into arterioles. These, in turn, divide to form capillaries, so tiny that they can be seen only with a microscope. So extensive is the capillary network that every body cell is close to a capillary. The wall of the capillary is just one cell thick, and it is quite 'leaky'. Liquid carrying oxygen and food leaks out of capillaries, supplies the cells and collects their waste, and flows back into the blood in the capillaries. Capillaries join to form venules, which in turn link up to form larger and larger veins.

HEART STRUCTURE

The heart is at the centre of the circulatory system. It is a hollow organ with walls made mainly of muscle.

The heart works as a pump to push blood around the twin circuits of the circulatory system. In fact, it is actually two pumps joined together. If we look inside the heart we can see its structure and how the two pumps – right and left – fit together.

The heart has four sections or chambers. The two upper chambers are called atria (one is called an atrium). The two lower chambers are called ventricles. The right atrium and ventricle form one pump, while the left atrium and ventricle form the other. Valves between each atrium and ventricle, and between each ventricle and the blood vessel that leaves it, make sure that blood flows in only one direction.

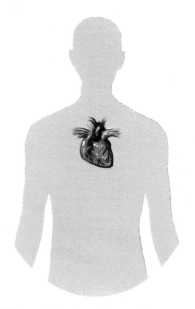

Where is the heart?
Your heart is in your chest. It tips slightly to the left-hand side of your body.

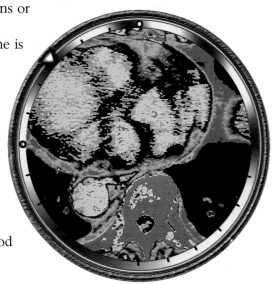

Body slice
This picture was produced by a machine called a CT scanner. The image it provides shows a 'slice' through the chest. The heart and its blood vessels are coloured yellow, the lungs blue, and the backbone pink.

Outside view
The fist-sized heart is located in the chest between the two lungs. Both lungs and heart are surrounded by a protective cage formed by the ribs. A tough layer called the pericardium surrounds and protects the heart. The pericardium has a number of layers, two of which have slippery surfaces. As the heart beats these surfaces slide over each other, making sure that the heart does not rub or catch – something that would be very painful – against any of the surrounding parts of the body.

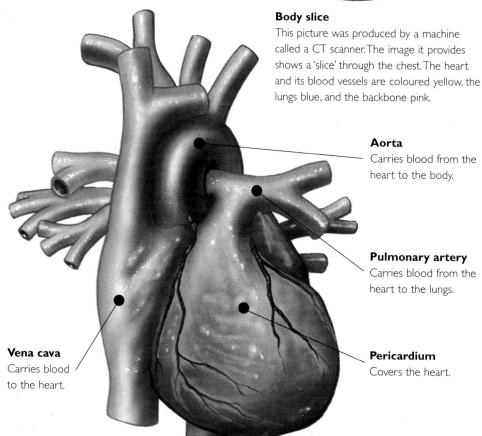

Aorta
Carries blood from the heart to the body.

Pulmonary artery
Carries blood from the heart to the lungs.

Pericardium
Covers the heart.

Vena cava
Carries blood to the heart.

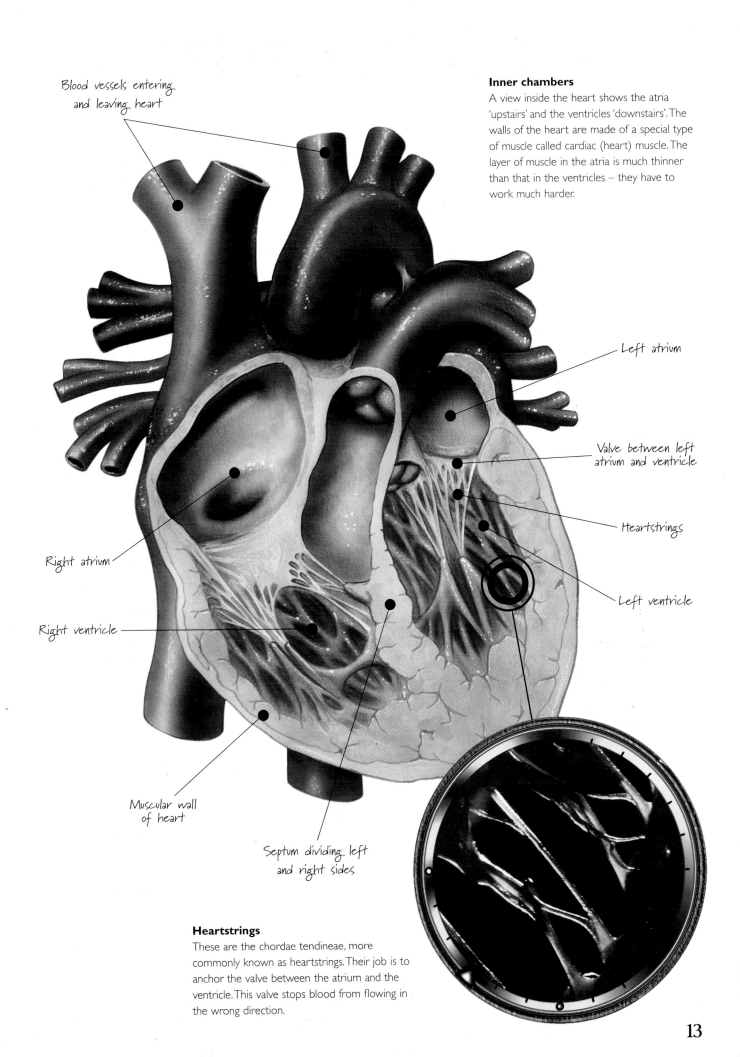

Blood vessels entering and leaving heart

Inner chambers
A view inside the heart shows the atria 'upstairs' and the ventricles 'downstairs'. The walls of the heart are made of a special type of muscle called cardiac (heart) muscle. The layer of muscle in the atria is much thinner than that in the ventricles – they have to work much harder.

Left atrium

Valve between left atrium and ventricle

Heartstrings

Right atrium

Left ventricle

Right ventricle

Muscular wall of heart

Septum dividing left and right sides

Heartstrings
These are the chordae tendineae, more commonly known as heartstrings. Their job is to anchor the valve between the atrium and the ventricle. This valve stops blood from flowing in the wrong direction.

THE LIVING PUMP

The heart is a living pump that lasts for a lifetime. It tirelessly contracts (squeezes) to push blood around the body between 60 and 70 times a minute, 10,000 times a day, and over 2 billion times during a person's life.

It can pump ceaselessly without rest because of the cardiac muscle in its walls. Cardiac muscle can contract repeatedly without tiring. The muscles that move your arms and legs cannot do this. Try opening and closing your fist once a second – the same rate as the heart beats – and see how long it is before your arm and hand muscles tire and you have to give up.

The heart has already been described as two pumps in one. Let's look at the right-hand pump first of all. Deoxygenated blood – blood low in oxygen – enters the right atrium from two big veins. These are the superior (upper) vena cava and inferior (lower) vena cava. This blood passes from the right atrium into the right ventricle. The right ventricle contracts to pump blood along the pulmonary arteries to the two lungs.

Now the left-hand pump. Oxygenated blood – blood newly filled with oxygen in the lungs – enters the left atrium through the pulmonary veins. It then passes to the left ventricle, which pumps it out of the heart along the aorta.

Semilunar valve
Semilunar valves guard the exits from the heart. One lies between the left ventricle and the aorta; the other between the right ventricle and the pulmonary vein. Both ensure that blood does not flow backwards into the heart.

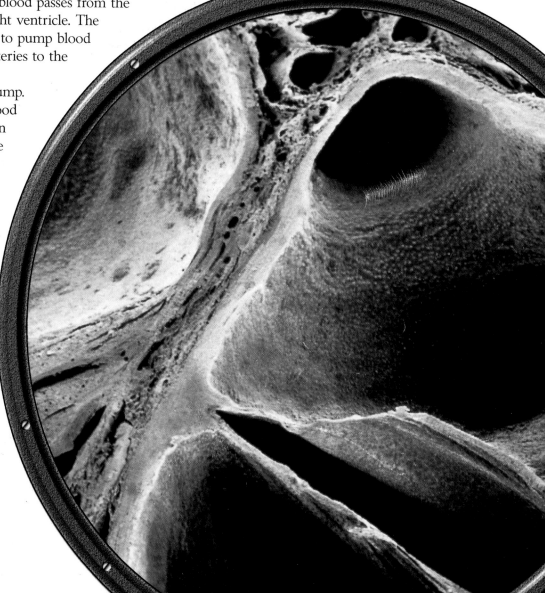

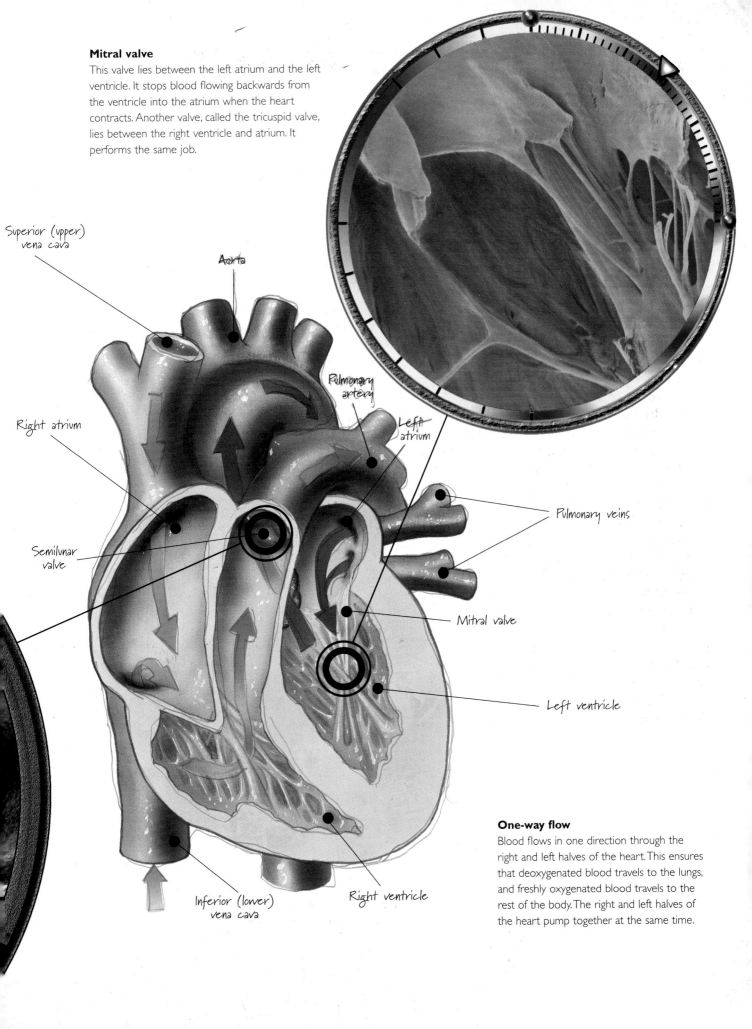

Mitral valve
This valve lies between the left atrium and the left ventricle. It stops blood flowing backwards from the ventricle into the atrium when the heart contracts. Another valve, called the tricuspid valve, lies between the right ventricle and atrium. It performs the same job.

Superior (upper) vena cava

Aorta

Right atrium

Semilunar valve

Pulmonary artery

Left atrium

Pulmonary veins

Mitral valve

Left ventricle

Inferior (lower) vena cava

Right ventricle

One-way flow
Blood flows in one direction through the right and left halves of the heart. This ensures that deoxygenated blood travels to the lungs, and freshly oxygenated blood travels to the rest of the body. The right and left halves of the heart pump together at the same time.

15

HEARTBEAT CYCLE

Every time the heart contracts or beats, the right side pumps blood to the lungs and the left side pumps blood to the body. A heartbeat is not a single action, however. It is made up of different stages during which the heart first fills with blood and then pumps it out.

The same stages are repeated again and again. This is called a cycle because it keeps going round and round. At the top of the heart is a tiny area called the sino-atrial node, that sets the pace that the rest of the heart follows. To start each heartbeat cycle, the pacemaker sends out electrical signals that make the muscle cells in the heart wall contract. Because electrical signals spread down through first the atria, and then the ventricles, the chambers contract in the correct sequence to make the heart pump properly.

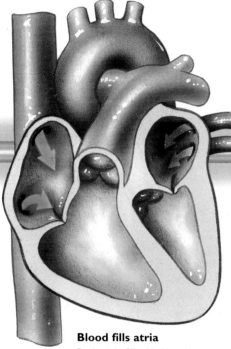

Blood fills atria
Both atria fill with blood, some of which also flows into the ventricles. This is called diastole – both atria and ventricles are relaxed (not contracting).

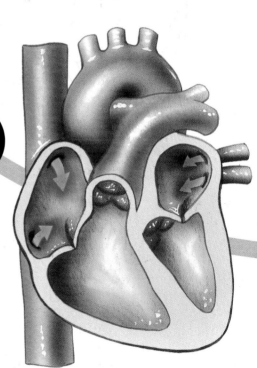

The ventricles relax
The ventricles relax and the heart enters diastole once more. The semilunar valves that guard the heart's exit through the aorta and pulmonary artery close. This stops blood flowing the wrong way back into the ventricles.

Electrical signals

The electrical signals produced by the pacemaker can be picked up by a machine called an electrocardiograph. This produces a trace called an ECG (electrocardiogram), which records the electrical changes that occur during the heartbeat cycle. ECGs are also used to see if there is anything wrong with the heart.

3

2

2

4

3

Blood fills ventricles

Both atria contract (squeeze) at the same time. This is called atrial systole, and it pushes blood through into the ventricles. Notice that atria have much thinner walls than ventricles because they only have to push blood a short distance.

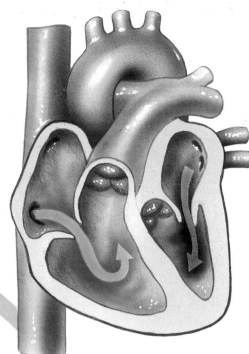

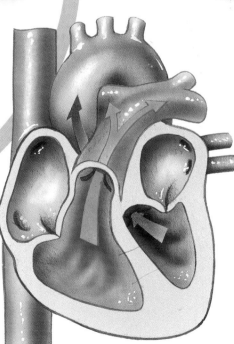

Ventricles contract to pump blood

Both ventricles contract at the same time. This is called ventricular systole and it pushes blood out of the heart to the lungs and body. This action forces the tricuspid and bicuspid valves to close, so stopping the blood from flowing back to the atria. Notice that the left ventricle has a thicker wall than the right because it has to pump blood to all parts of the body. The right ventricle only has to pump blood to the lungs, which are just next door to the heart.

THE HEART AT WORK

Pulse rate and blood pressure are two external signs that tell us the heart is at work. A pulse occurs every time the heart beats. A surge of pressure passes down the arteries. This makes their elastic walls at first expand and then bounce back. This is the pulse, and it can be felt most easily where the artery is both near the surface of the skin and passes over a bone.

A good place to feel a pulse is in the wrist. The number of pulses felt in a minute is called the pulse rate and, of course, this is the same as the heart rate.

To keep working, the heart requires a blood supply of its own. This may seem a bit odd at first because of the large amount of blood that actually passes through the heart every minute. However, the blood pumped by the heart cannot possibly reach every single heart muscle cell, and these cells require a constant supply of food and oxygen. This is provided by the coronary blood supply.

Finding your pulse

Find your pulse by pressing two fingers down on your wrist, as shown here. If you count the number of pulses for 15 seconds, and multiply that number by four, it will give you your pulse rate.

Exercise and heart rate

Pulse rate – and heart rate – are constantly changing. For example, exercise increases your heart rate. The muscles that move you are working hard and need more food and oxygen. This graph shows that when you start exercising, the heart beats faster to keep up with the muscles' demands. Afterwards, heart rate gradually returns to normal.

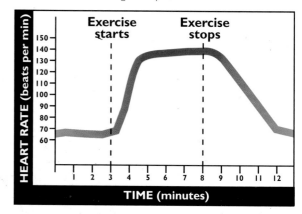

18

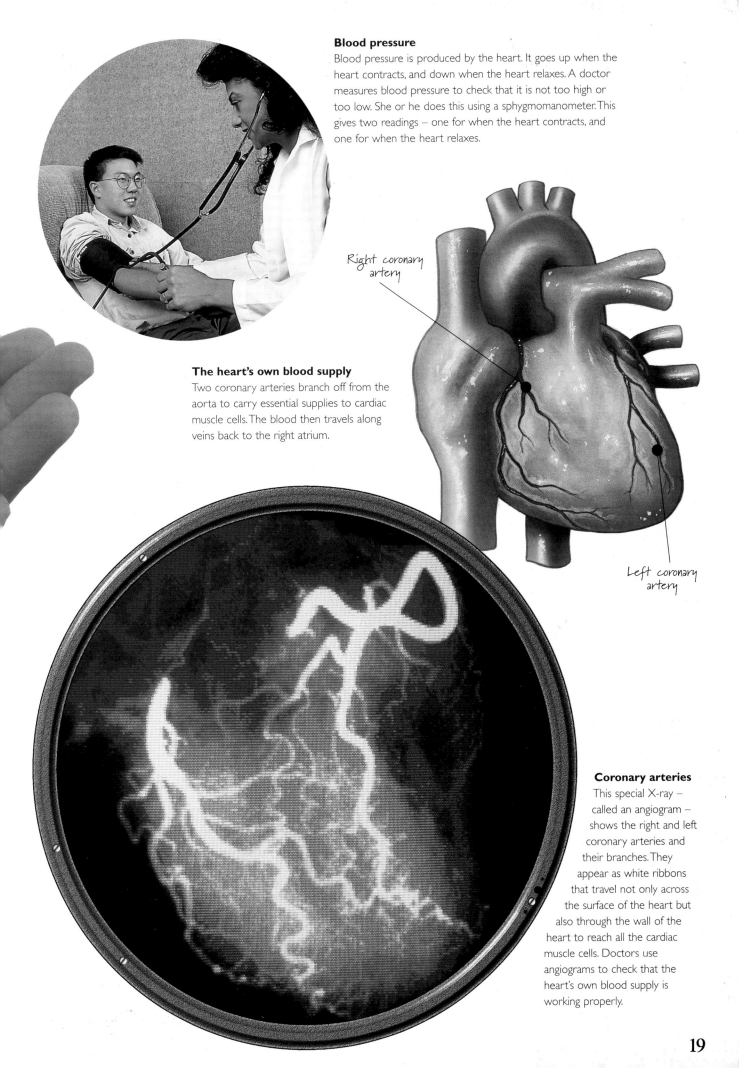

Blood pressure

Blood pressure is produced by the heart. It goes up when the heart contracts, and down when the heart relaxes. A doctor measures blood pressure to check that it is not too high or too low. She or he does this using a sphygmomanometer. This gives two readings – one for when the heart contracts, and one for when the heart relaxes.

The heart's own blood supply

Two coronary arteries branch off from the aorta to carry essential supplies to cardiac muscle cells. The blood then travels along veins back to the right atrium.

Right coronary artery

Left coronary artery

Coronary arteries

This special X-ray – called an angiogram – shows the right and left coronary arteries and their branches. They appear as white ribbons that travel not only across the surface of the heart but also through the wall of the heart to reach all the cardiac muscle cells. Doctors use angiograms to check that the heart's own blood supply is working properly.

WHAT IS BLOOD?

If you cut your finger, what do you see? A trickle of blood — a red liquid, thicker than water, and slightly salty to the taste. But there is more to blood than meets the eye.

Blood is not just a simple liquid. The 5 litres (8.8 pints) or so of blood circulating around an adult's body consists of billions of living blood cells floating in a liquid called plasma.

If a small sample of blood is poured into a test tube and put in a machine called a centrifuge it can be spun round and round at very high speed. When this happens, the different parts of the blood separate out into layers. The heavier, solid parts — the blood cells — are pushed to the bottom of the tube. The lighter, liquid part — the plasma remains at the top. If blood is examined under a microscope, not one but several, different types of blood cells — red blood cells, white blood cells, and platelets — can be seen floating in plasma. Plasma itself is 95 per cent water; the rest of it is made up of dissolved substances, including salts — hence the salty taste!

Blood in a spin

Spinning blood in a centrifuge reveals its component parts. About 55 per cent consists of yellowish liquid plasma and 45 per cent of blood cells. Most blood cells are red blood cells; less than 1 per cent of blood is made up of white blood cells and platelets.

A unique tissue

Blood is unique because — unlike other tissues such as bone or cartilage — it is the body's only liquid tissue. Blood cells, floating suspended in plasma, course through arteries, veins, and capillaries pumped by the heart. As you can see, red blood cells far outnumber both white blood cells and platelets.

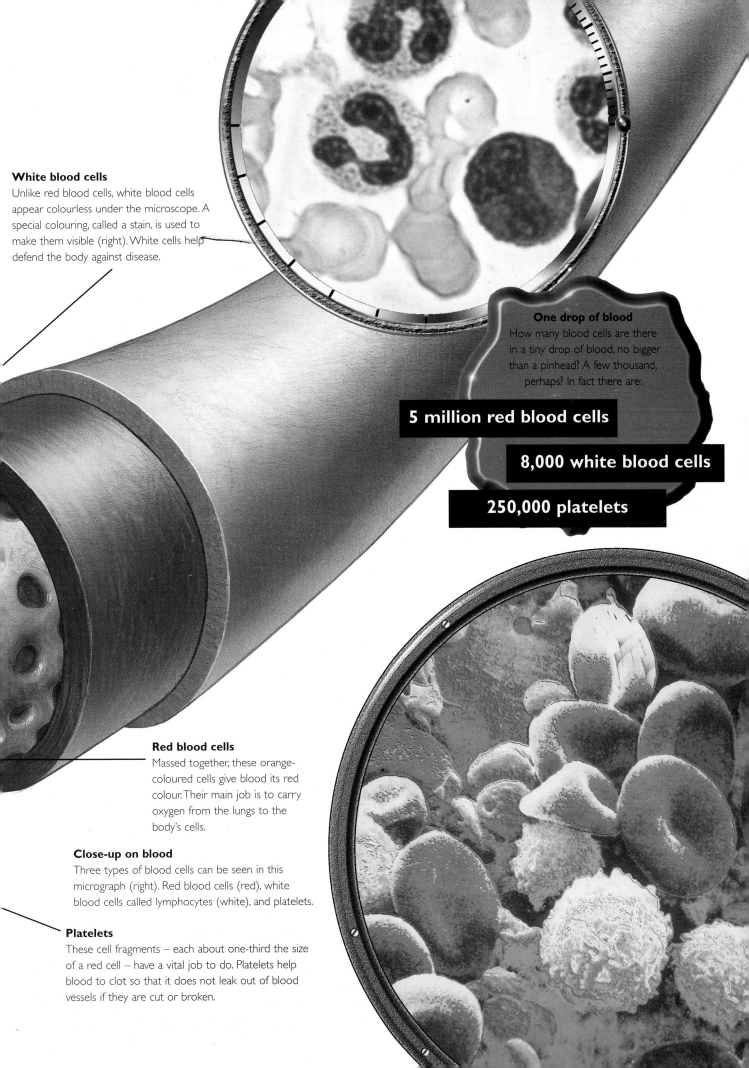

White blood cells

Unlike red blood cells, white blood cells appear colourless under the microscope. A special colouring, called a stain, is used to make them visible (right). White cells help defend the body against disease.

One drop of blood

How many blood cells are there in a tiny drop of blood, no bigger than a pinhead? A few thousand, perhaps? In fact there are:

5 million red blood cells

8,000 white blood cells

250,000 platelets

Red blood cells

Massed together, these orange-coloured cells give blood its red colour. Their main job is to carry oxygen from the lungs to the body's cells.

Close-up on blood

Three types of blood cells can be seen in this micrograph (right). Red blood cells (red), white blood cells called lymphocytes (white), and platelets.

Platelets

These cell fragments — each about one-third the size of a red cell — have a vital job to do. Platelets help blood to clot so that it does not leak out of blood vessels if they are cut or broken.

THE ROLE OF BLOOD

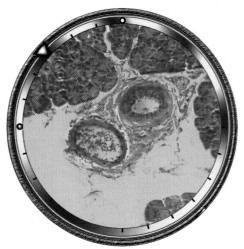

Artery and vein

An artery (right) and a vein (left) run side by side. This micrograph shows them cut open across their width so that each vessel appears like a circle. Veins and arteries carry blood around the body.

Modern life depends on transport to deliver our food and fuel, and to collect our rubbish and dispose of it. The same is true of the body and blood. Without blood circulating around it, and carrying materials to and from the body's billions of cells, the human body could not survive.

Most materials transported by the blood are carried in the plasma, the liquid part of the blood. These include nutrients (food), waste substances such as urea and carbon dioxide, and chemical messengers called hormones.

Red blood cells have a transport role as well. They carry oxygen from the lungs to all body cells, where it is used during respiration. This is the process that releases essential energy from glucose.

Carbon dioxide, released as a waste product of respiration, is poisonous to the body. It is carried – partly by red blood cells and partly dissolved in plasma – to the lungs, where it is breathed out.

Finally, blood transports the heat generated in all tissues, but especially in the liver and the muscles. It 'spreads out' the heat, and helps to keep the body temperature steady, at around 37 degrees Centigrade (98.6 degrees Fahrenheit).

Transport routes

Blood transports many different things. Here you can see what the blood transports, and where it picks up and makes its deliveries.

Oxygen

Oxygen is carried from the lungs – where it enters the body from the air when you breathe in – to all body cells.

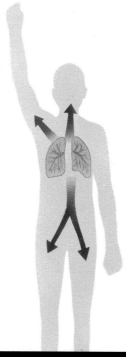

Waste

Waste carbon dioxide is produced by all body cells and is carried by the blood to the lungs, where it passes into the air you breathe out. Another waste carried by the blood is urea, made in the liver and carried to the kidneys, where it passes out in urine.

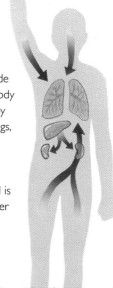

OXYGEN

WASTE

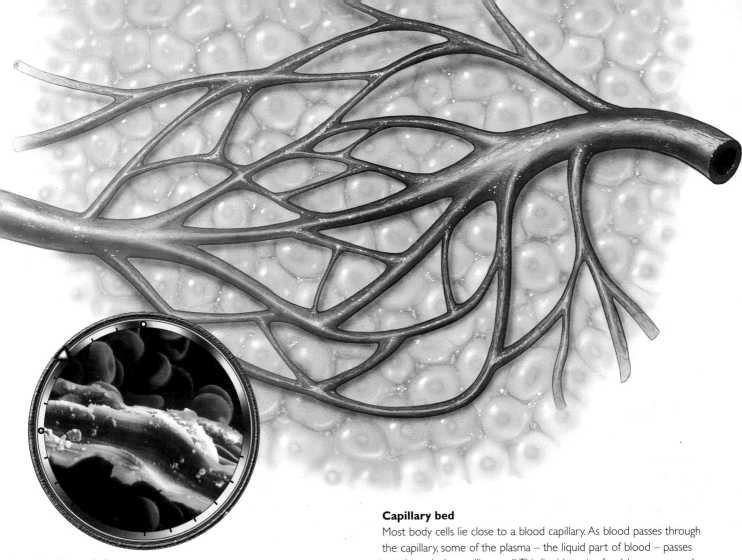

Capillary delivery

A tiny capillary is shown split open here. Notice that it is only just wider than the red blood cells that have spilled out of it.

Capillary bed

Most body cells lie close to a blood capillary. As blood passes through the capillary, some of the plasma – the liquid part of blood – passes out through the capillary wall. This liquid carries food, hormones and oxygen to each and every cell in the body. At the same time, the plasma picks up wastes and re-enters the blood in the capillary to be carried back towards the heart.

Nutrients

When you eat, food is digested and releases nutrients that are used by the body. These nutrients are absorbed from the small intestine into the bloodstream and are carried to all body cells.

Hormones

Hormones are chemical messengers that are released into the bloodstream from glands called endocrine glands. The blood carries hormones to target cells, where they trigger changes in the way the body works.

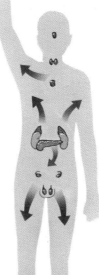

Heat

Heat is released by all cells. Some parts of the body – especially the liver and muscles – produce a lot of heat because they work so hard. Blood distributes heat around the body so that all its parts are kept warm – even toes and fingers!

NUTRIENTS　　　HORMONES　　　HEAT

RED BLOOD CELLS

Doughnut shape
A section through a red blood cell reveals its dimpled disc — or doughnut shape. This shape provides the cell with a large area of surface for taking in oxygen molecules.

Red blood cells are the body's oxygen carriers. They make the round trip from lungs to tissues and back about once every minute. Unlike all the other cells in your body, red blood cells have no nucleus (control centre). Instead, each doughnut-shaped cell is basically a 'bag' packed with molecules of a substance called haemoglobin, that gives the cell its red colour.

Haemoglobin is a special type of protein that picks up oxygen where it is plentiful, and releases it where it is scarce. So, as a red blood cell passes through the lungs — where oxygen is taken into the body — its haemoglobin molecules load up with oxygen. The oxygen-haemoglobin combination, called oxyhaemoglobin, makes the blood cells, and the blood, bright red. This is the colour of blood found in the arteries.

When a red blood cell passes through the tissues — where body cells constantly use up oxygen in order to release energy and stay alive — its haemoglobin molecules unload their oxygen. Unloaded haemoglobin makes blood cells, and blood, darker red. This is the colour found in the veins. Red blood cells also carry some carbon dioxide, a waste material produced by cells, although most carbon dioxide is carried in the plasma.

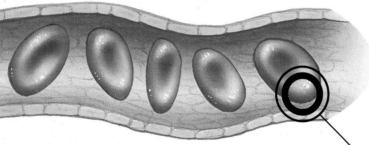

In a queue
The diameter of a red blood cell is about the same as that of a capillary. When picking up oxygen in the lungs — or unloading it in the tissues — red blood cells move slowly and in single file. This makes loading and unloading oxygen more efficient.

Oxygen carrier
Every red blood cell is packed with nearly 250 million haemoglobin molecules. Each haemoglobin molecule can pick up and carry four molecules of oxygen. This means that every time a fully-loaded red blood cell travels from the lungs to the tissues it is carrying about one billion (thousand million) oxygen molecules.

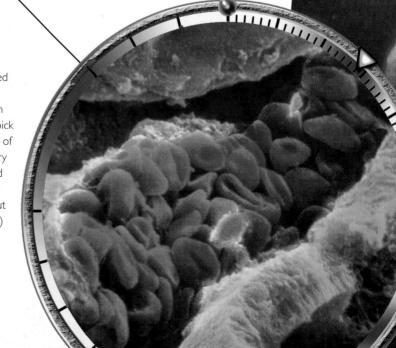

Red blood cells

Ninety-nine per cent of the cells in your
blood are red blood cells. That's an incredible
25 trillion (million million) cells altogether.

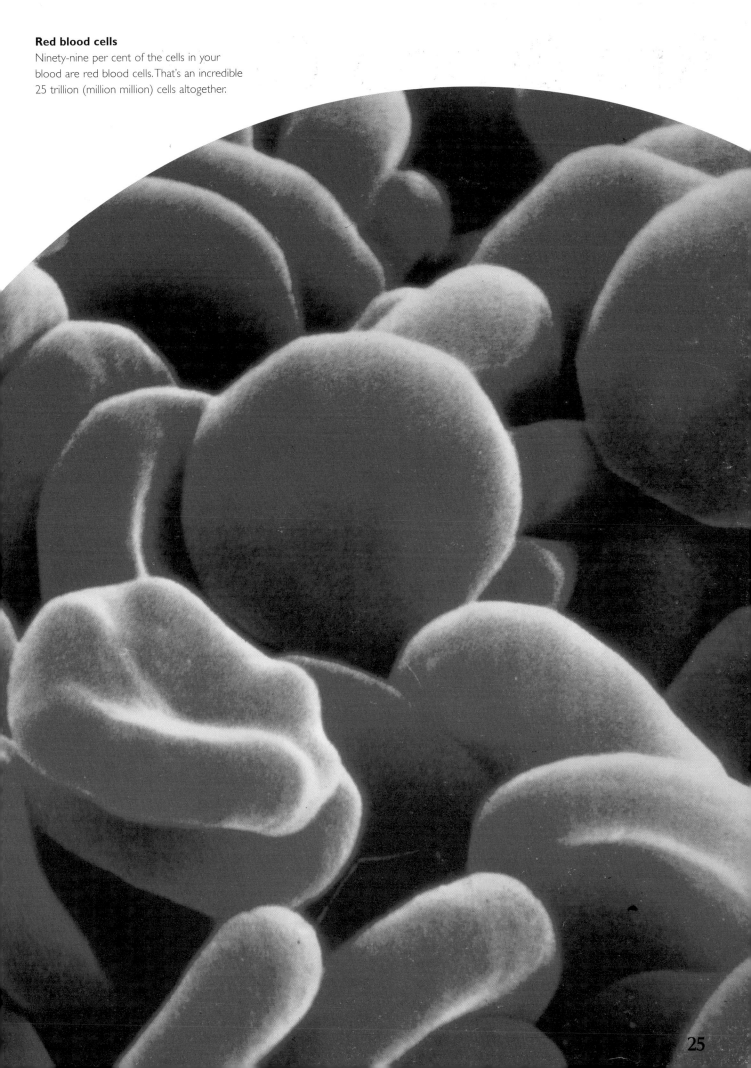

WHITE BLOOD CELLS & PLATELETS

There are far fewer white blood cells than the oxygen-carrying red blood cells, but that does not mean they are any less important. White blood cells form a mobile defence force that protects the body from damage by invaders.

These include all types of germs such as viruses, bacteria, and fungi that enter the body through the mouth or cuts in the skin. White blood cells also help protect us by destroying cancer cells − body cells that start behaving abnormally and multiplying out of control.

While red blood cells are confined to the blood vessels, white blood cells are able to change shape and squeeze in and out through the walls of capillaries. Once in the surrounding tissues, they can carry out search-and-destroy missions, attacking germs and infected cells.

There are three main types of white blood cells: neutrophils, lymphocytes and monocytes. The last two types are also found in another part of the body's defence system − the lymphatic system. Platelets are not really cells, but are fragments of cells. They play a vital part in the process that makes the blood clot, and stop it from leaking out if blood vessels under the skin are damaged.

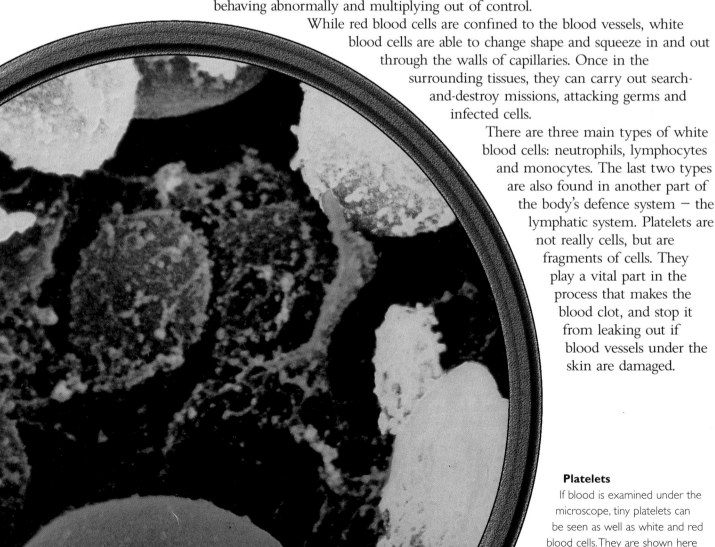

Platelets

If blood is examined under the microscope, tiny platelets can be seen as well as white and red blood cells. They are shown here in yellow. Platelets are flattened cell fragments. They play a vital role in plugging leaks in broken blood vessels.

Blood cell army

From front to back, this micrograph shows one platelet, one white blood cell and two red blood cells. They represent, in one picture, the cells that are found in everyone's blood, suspended in liquid plasma.

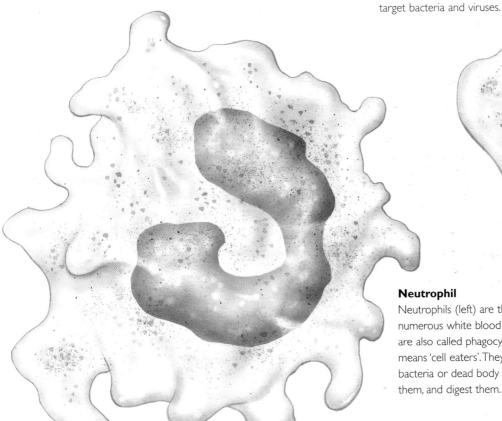

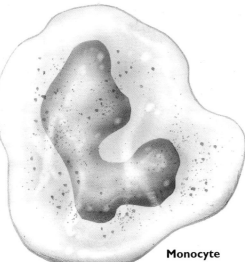

Monocyte

Monocytes (above) appear in large numbers when a part of the body becomes infected. They wander through the infected tissue and, like neutrophils, they eat up germs and other foreign particles.

Lymphocyte

Lymphocytes (below, right) form the chemical warfare branch of the body's defence force. They release killer chemicals called antibodies that target bacteria and viruses.

Neutrophil

Neutrophils (left) are the most numerous white blood cells. They are also called phagocytes, which means 'cell eaters'. They surround bacteria or dead body cells, engulf them, and digest them.

CLOTTING AND HEALING

If your skin gets cut and a blood vessel is punctured some blood will escape, but the flow is soon stemmed. The reason? The body has a remarkable self-repair system that stops blood being lost from a damaged blood vessel, and then allows the wound to heal.

Let's imagine that you have stuck a pin in your finger, and the pin has made a hole in a blood vessel. What happens next? Platelets gather at the wound and stick to each other, forming a plug that helps to block the hole. Then clotting begins. Substances released by blood plasma, the damaged cells and the sticky platelets, form special chemicals called clotting factors. These produce hair-like strands of fibrin in the blood. The fibrin strands trap red blood cells and make the blood thicker. This is a clot. Eventually the outer surface of the clot dries to form a protective scab. This protects the wound from infection as it heals. Internal wounds heal in the same way, but without a scab.

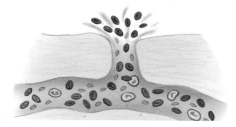

The wound bleeds
When skin is cut and a blood vessel is punctured, blood is lost. Platelets quickly collect at the wound site and stick together to form a plug. If the hole is small, the plug may be enough to stop the leak.

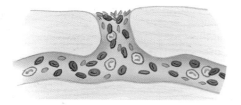

The blood clots
There is a substance called fibrinogen that is dissolved in blood plasma. At the wound site, clotting factors turn fibrinogen into threads of fibrin, which traps cells and forms a clot of thick blood. White blood cells move in to eat up any invading bacteria.

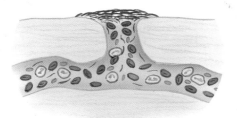

A scab is formed
The clot dries in the air to form a hard, crusty scab. The scab remains in place until all the tissues beneath it have been repaired. The natural healing process is complete.

Sticky platelets
Normally platelets float freely in blood plasma. But as soon as a blood vessel breaks, platelets change. They swell up, become spiky, and stick together to make a plug.

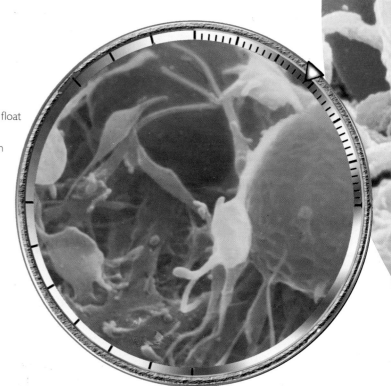

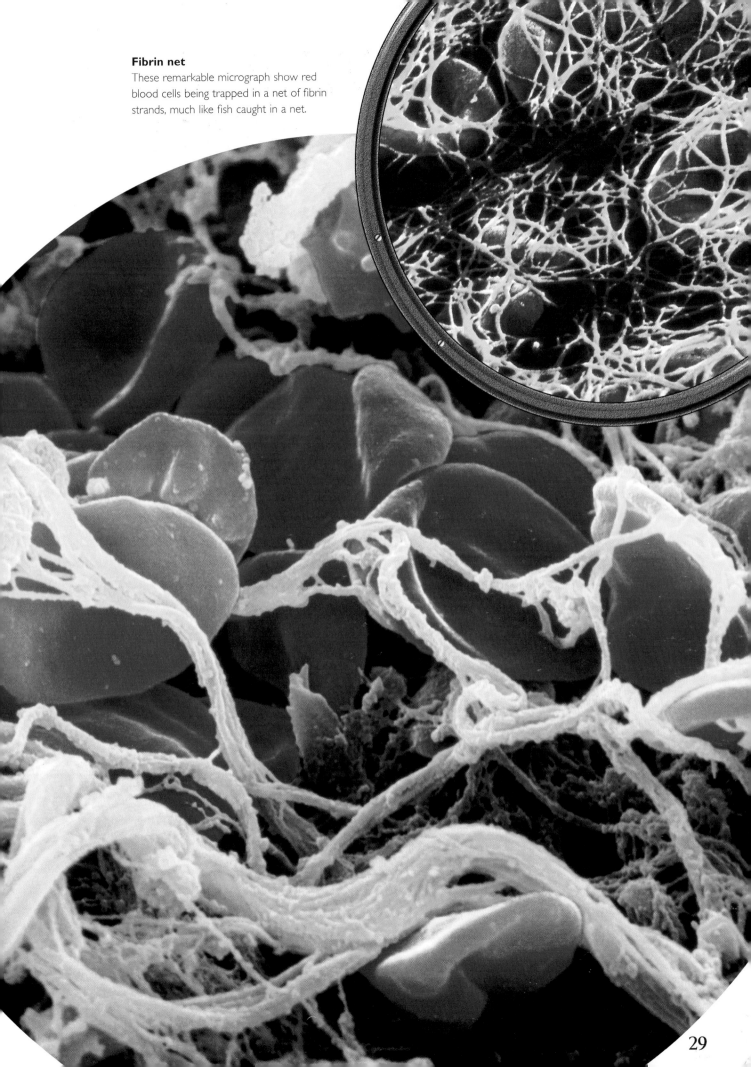

Fibrin net
These remarkable micrograph show red blood cells being trapped in a net of fibrin strands, much like fish caught in a net.

THE BLOOD CELL FACTORY

Blood cells don't last forever. In time, they get 'worn out' and have to be replaced with new ones. New red and white blood cells are manufactured in the jelly-like red marrow that is found in the middle of some of the body's bones.

Red blood cells last for about 120 days. After being repeatedly battered on countless trips round the body, they become fragile. Their haemoglobin starts to disintegrate as well, so they can no longer carry oxygen properly. Old red blood cells are deposited in the 'scrap yards' of the spleen and liver where they are broken up. Useful parts, such as iron, are recycled for making new cells. As one red blood cell is removed, another is produced. An incredible two million red blood cells are produced by the bone marrow every single second. Many white blood cells last for a few weeks, although some will last for just hours if they are busy dealing with a sudden invasion of germs. Lymphocytes, on the other hand, are white blood cells that can survive for years, always ready to attack specific germs.

Bone marrow

Production line

Blood cells of all types are the 'descendants' of a single type of 'grandmother' cell. It is called a haemocytoblast (this long word just means 'blood cell producer'). Haemocytoblasts divide to produce a number of different types of 'mother' cells. These, in turn, divide rapidly to produce millions of 'offspring' – red blood cells and the different types of white blood cells. When these cells are mature ('grown up') they migrate from bone marrow into blood capillaries and enter the bloodstream to begin their different jobs.

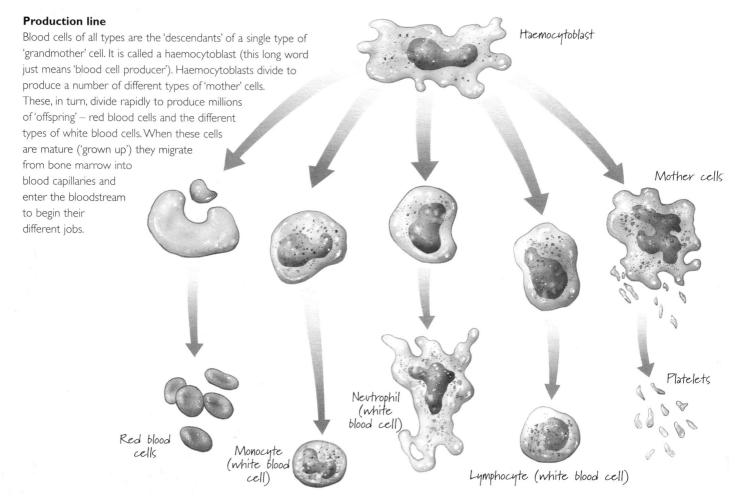

Haemocytoblast

Mother cells

Red blood cells

Monocyte (white blood cell)

Neutrophil (white blood cell)

Lymphocyte (white blood cell)

Platelets

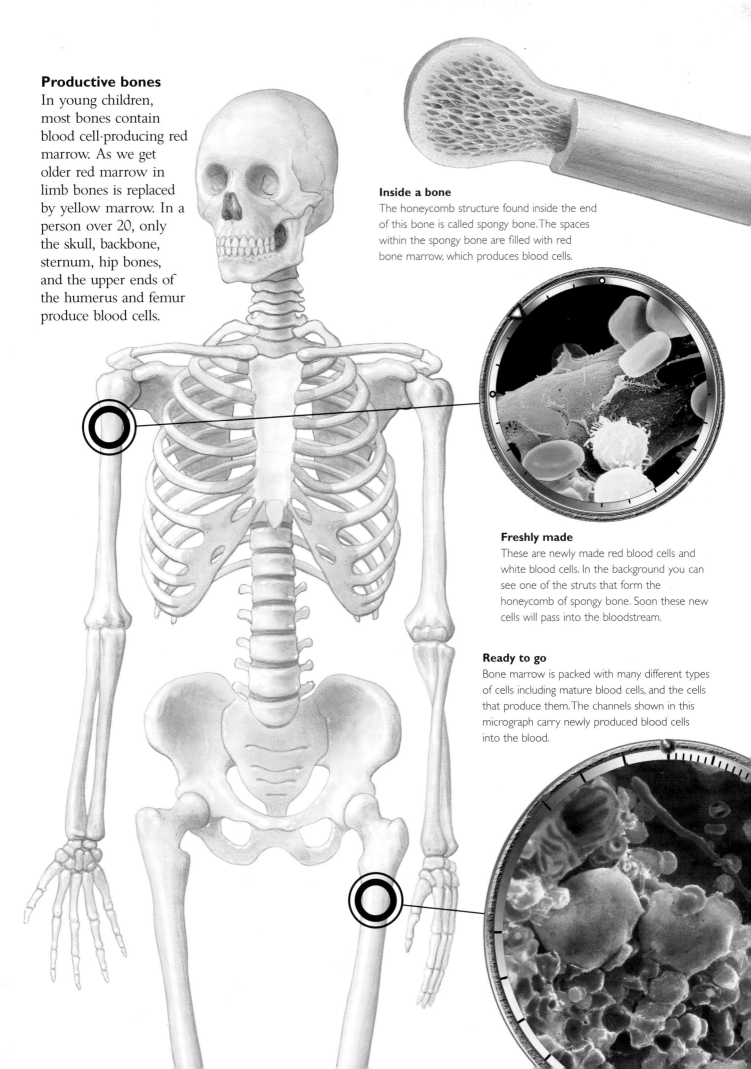

Productive bones

In young children, most bones contain blood cell-producing red marrow. As we get older red marrow in limb bones is replaced by yellow marrow. In a person over 20, only the skull, backbone, sternum, hip bones, and the upper ends of the humerus and femur produce blood cells.

Inside a bone

The honeycomb structure found inside the end of this bone is called spongy bone. The spaces within the spongy bone are filled with red bone marrow, which produces blood cells.

Freshly made

These are newly made red blood cells and white blood cells. In the background you can see one of the struts that form the honeycomb of spongy bone. Soon these new cells will pass into the bloodstream.

Ready to go

Bone marrow is packed with many different types of cells including mature blood cells, and the cells that produce them. The channels shown in this micrograph carry newly produced blood cells into the blood.

THE LYMPHATIC SYSTEM

Blood vessels are not the only tubes running around the body. There is another system of vessels called lymphatic vessels that range in size from microscopic lymph capillaries to much larger lymph channels. Lymphatic vessels form part of the lymphatic system. To understand what this does we need to return to the circulatory system.

As blood passes through the tiny blood capillaries, fluid leaks out from the capillaries into the surrounding tissues. It does this in order to supply cells with food and oxygen. Most of the fluid returns immediately to the blood but some does not. This excess fluid has to be channelled back into the bloodstream, or parts of the body would expand rather like a balloon, and the blood would become too thick and concentrated.

This is where the lymphatic system comes into action. It acts as a drainage system. Excess fluid passes into the lymph capillaries that reach every part of the body. This clear watery fluid, now called lymph, travels one way into larger and larger vessels that finally join to form ducts that empty the lymph back into the blood where it belongs.

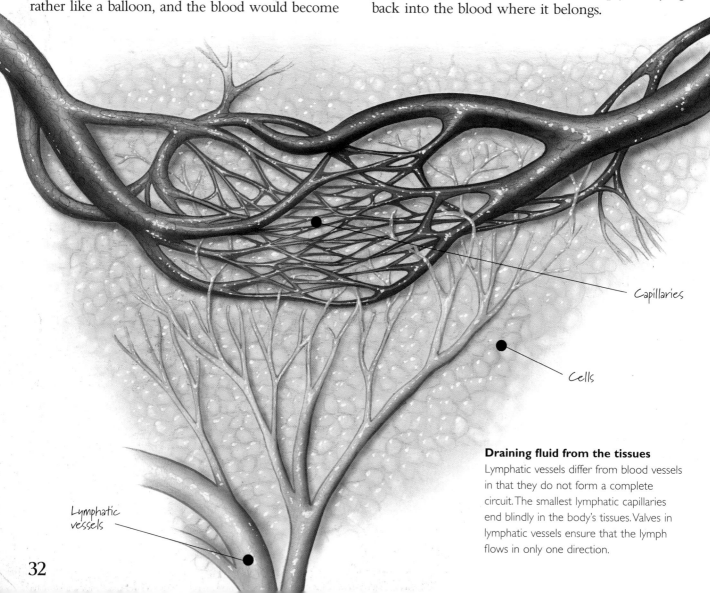

Capillaries

Cells

Lymphatic vessels

Draining fluid from the tissues
Lymphatic vessels differ from blood vessels in that they do not form a complete circuit. The smallest lymphatic capillaries end blindly in the body's tissues. Valves in lymphatic vessels ensure that the lymph flows in only one direction.

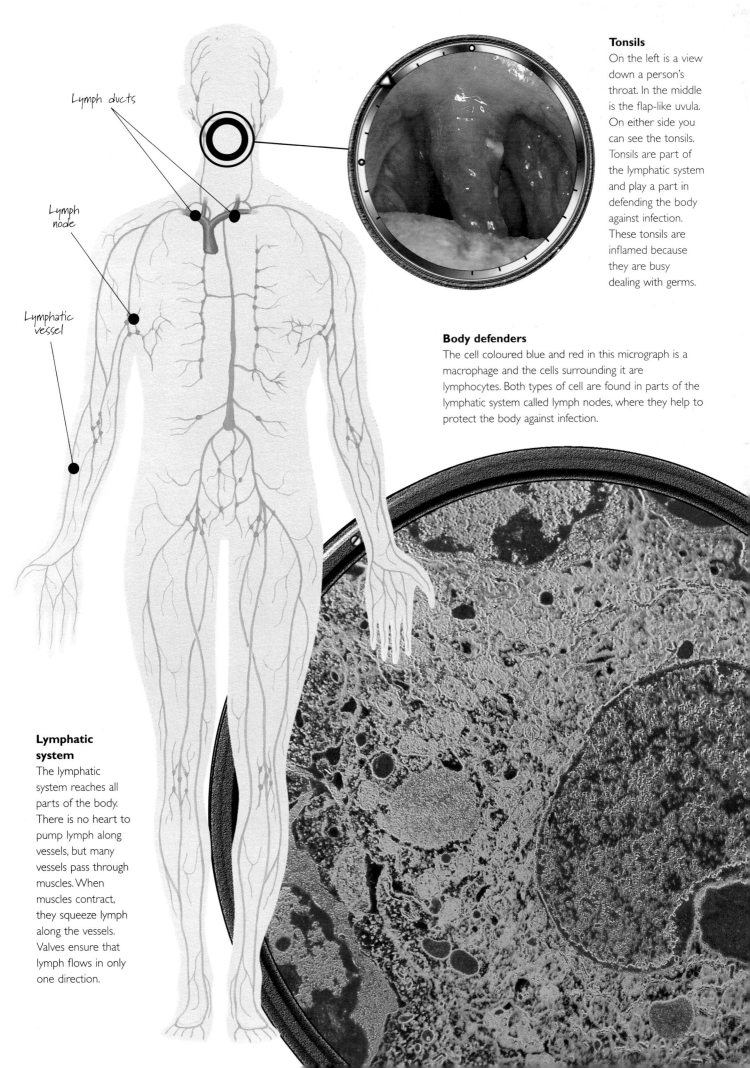

Lymph ducts

Lymph node

Lymphatic vessel

Tonsils

On the left is a view down a person's throat. In the middle is the flap-like uvula. On either side you can see the tonsils. Tonsils are part of the lymphatic system and play a part in defending the body against infection. These tonsils are inflamed because they are busy dealing with germs.

Body defenders

The cell coloured blue and red in this micrograph is a macrophage and the cells surrounding it are lymphocytes. Both types of cell are found in parts of the lymphatic system called lymph nodes, where they help to protect the body against infection.

Lymphatic system

The lymphatic system reaches all parts of the body. There is no heart to pump lymph along vessels, but many vessels pass through muscles. When muscles contract, they squeeze lymph along the vessels. Valves ensure that lymph flows in only one direction.

LYMPH NODES

The lymphatic system drains excess fluid from the tissues. It has another important function. Dotted throughout the lymphatic system are bean-shaped swellings called lymph nodes. Lymph nodes play a vital role in defending the body against disease.

As lymph passes through the lymph nodes on its journey back to the blood, germs and debris present in the lymph are filtered out and destroyed. Cells inside the lymph nodes called macrophages – similar to monocytes in the blood – attack and eat germs. Other cells called lymphocytes – like the lymphocytes in the blood – release killer chemicals called antibodies, which target and destroy specific germs. Macrophages and lymphocytes are made in the bone marrow and in the lymphatic system itself.

In addition to the lymph nodes, the lymphatic system has other organs that help in the body's defence. These include the spleen and the tonsils.

Lymph nodes
Lymph nodes are found all over the body, but are most numerous in the neck, armpit, and groin. If lymph nodes become swollen – this is often called swollen glands – it is an indication that they are busy fighting an infection.

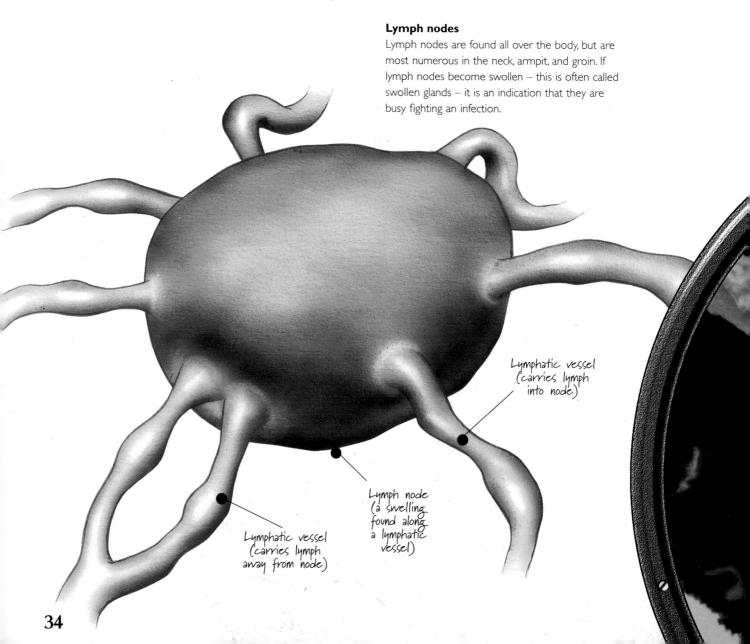

Lymphatic vessel (carries lymph into node)

Lymph node (a swelling found along a lymphatic vessel)

Lymphatic vessel (carries lymph away from node)

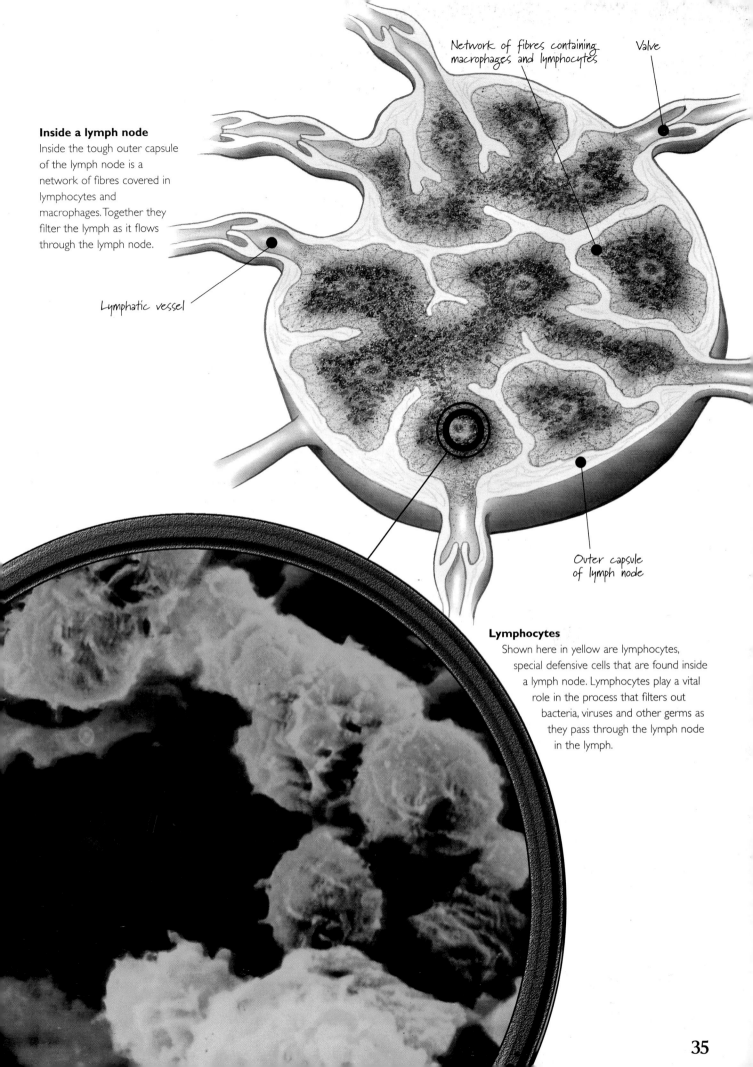

Inside a lymph node

Inside the tough outer capsule of the lymph node is a network of fibres covered in lymphocytes and macrophages. Together they filter the lymph as it flows through the lymph node.

Lymphatic vessel

Network of fibres containing macrophages and lymphocytes

Valve

Outer capsule of lymph node

Lymphocytes

Shown here in yellow are lymphocytes, special defensive cells that are found inside a lymph node. Lymphocytes play a vital role in the process that filters out bacteria, viruses and other germs as they pass through the lymph node in the lymph.

THE IMMUNE SYSTEM

On patrol
This blue and green cell is a macrophage on the move. Macrophages migrate through the body's tissues in search of bacteria and other germs and debris, which they surround, suck in, and then digest.

The human body is constantly under attack from invaders. These are microscopic germs, such as bacteria and viruses. They are found in the air we breathe, in the water we drink, the food we eat, and even on the people we touch. If allowed to multiply inside the body, germs will cause disease.

The body has to defend itself against infection by any and all germs. If it does not, germs will take over the body and kill it. Fortunately, each of us has a highly effective system of defence against germs. It is called the immune system. The immune system consists of cells found mainly in the blood and lymphatic systems.

If bacteria or viruses manage to get through the body's first line of defence – such as the germ-proof skin – they are attacked by phagocytes – 'cell eaters' – that include neutrophils and macrophages. At the same time the most sophisticated part of the immune system comes into action. Certain lymphocytes keep a record of each type of germ that enters the body. As soon as that type of germ tries to invade again, the lymphocyte recognizes it and releases antibodies to destroy it. That means that the person has become resistant – or immune – to that particular germ.

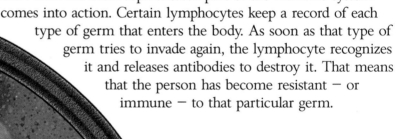

Star players
Lymphocytes are the star players of the immune system. Here you can see a lymphocyte (shown in blue) surrounding the spore of a fungus (in green) that has invaded the body. Unchecked, this fungus would spread and cause damage inside the body. Fortunately, the lymphocyte has caught it in time and is devouring its prey.

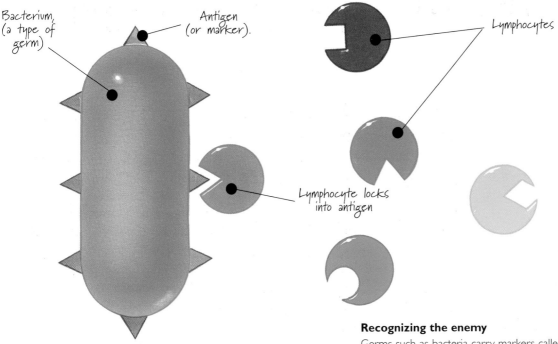

Bacterium (a type of germ)

Antigen (or marker).

Lymphocytes

Lymphocyte locks into antigen

Recognizing the enemy

Germs such as bacteria carry markers called antigens on their surface. Antigens enable lymphocytes to identify invading germs. Each lymphocyte recognizes a particular antigen, like a key fits a lock.

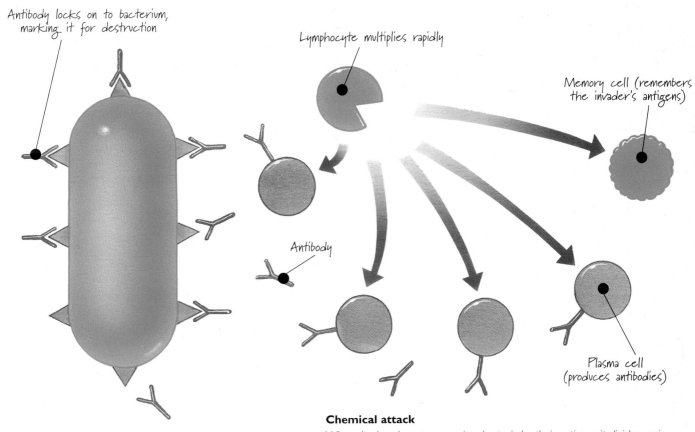

Antibody locks on to bacterium, marking it for destruction

Lymphocyte multiplies rapidly

Memory cell (remembers the invader's antigens)

Antibody

Plasma cell (produces antibodies)

Chemical attack

When the lymphocyte recognizes bacteria by their antigens, it divides again and again to produce two types of cells. Memory cells memorize the antigen, so that in any future invasion the body can react very quickly. Other cells, called plasma cells, make and release chemicals called antibodies. These target new invaders, locking on to their antigens. In this way they disable the invading bacterium, and mark it for destruction by other cells.

IMMUNIZATION

The immune system depends on cells called lymphocytes to recognize invading germs and immediately produce antibodies to destroy them.

This works very well when a germ enters the body many times, but what happens the first time a particular germ invades the body? In fact, it takes several days for lymphocytes to respond fully to the invader and produce enough antibody to destroy it. Some germs — such as the ones that cause polio — are so dangerous that in those few days they can cause serious illness or even kill. To give the immune system a helping hand, doctors use immunization, also called vaccination.

There are two types of immunization: active immunization and passive immunization. In active immunization the doctor injects the patient with germs that have been treated to stop them being dangerous. Although safe, they still cause lymphocytes to respond and keep a memory of the dangerous germ. If the person is then infected by the dangerous germ, the immune system instantly springs into action and destroys it. In passive immunization, the doctor injects the patient with antibodies against a particular germ, but protection does not last as long.

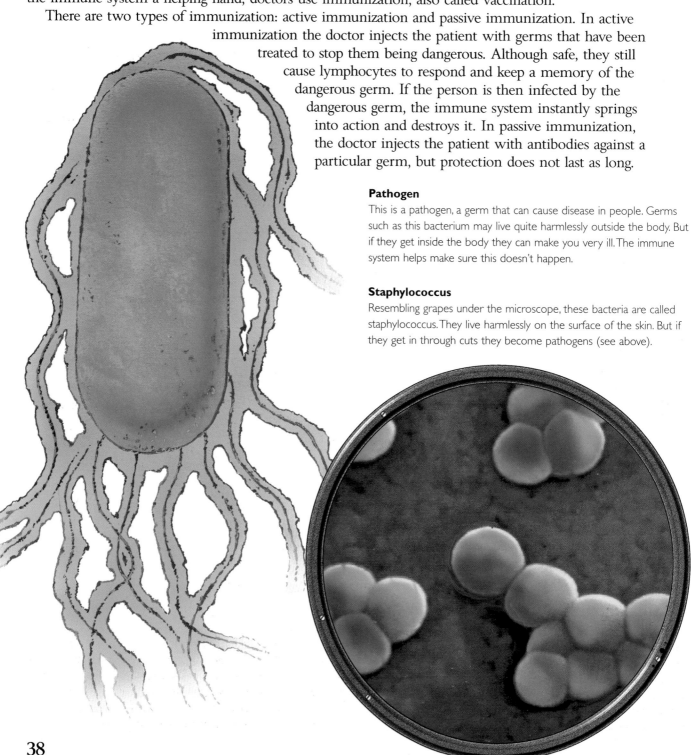

Pathogen
This is a pathogen, a germ that can cause disease in people. Germs such as this bacterium may live quite harmlessly outside the body. But if they get inside the body they can make you very ill. The immune system helps make sure this doesn't happen.

Staphylococcus
Resembling grapes under the microscope, these bacteria are called staphylococcus. They live harmlessly on the surface of the skin. But if they get in through cuts they become pathogens (see above).

Injecting vaccine

A person is injected with a harmless form of the pathogen, which does not cause the disease.

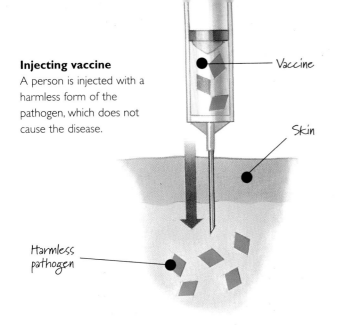

Vaccine

Skin

Harmless pathogen

Making serum

Blood is taken from a person or animal recovering from a disease. This blood contains antibodies to the disease.

Blood containing antibodies

Skin

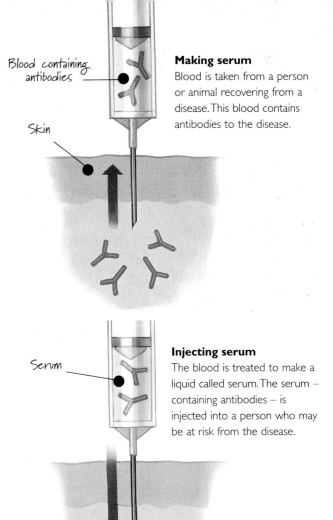

Injecting serum

The blood is treated to make a liquid called serum. The serum – containing antibodies – is injected into a person who may be at risk from the disease.

Serum

Antibodies

Antibodies are made

Although the pathogen is harmless, the body still recognizes it and makes antibodies against it.

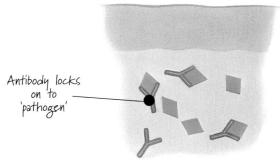

Antibody locks on to 'pathogen'

Fighting infection

If the body is invaded by the 'real' pathogen, the immune system responds immediately with huge numbers of antibodies to destroy the pathogen.

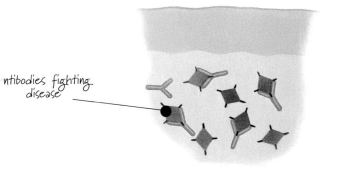

ntibodies fighting disease

Fighting infection

The antibodies get to work and destroy any pathogens that are inside the body.

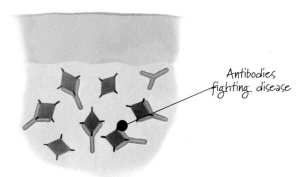

Antibodies fighting disease

Active immunization

This type of immunization uses a form of the pathogen – disease-causing germ such as bacteria or viruses – that has been slightly altered to stop it causing a disease. If it is injected into a person's body, they don't become ill, but they do produce antibodies against the pathogen that does cause disease. The body will do this every time it is threatened by that pathogen.

Passive immunization

This type of immunization uses a liquid called a serum that contains ready-made antibodies. Injected into the body, they act immediately to destroy a particular pathogen. But their effect is short-lived. They soon disappear. If the disease strikes again the body takes time to react and produce its own antibodies. This method is useful in the short term, but active immunization is better because it lasts longer.

BLOOD GROUPS

Samples of blood taken from different people may look the same, but they may not be identical. All blood contains the same things — plasma, red blood cells, white blood cells, and platelets. But there may be subtle differences between samples taken from different people, even from members of the same family.

Red blood cells carry tiny markers on their surface. These markers are called antigens. There are two types of antigen that a red blood cell can carry, and these are called A and B. So your red blood cells could carry antigen A, or antigen B, or both A and B, or no antigen at all.

The antigens divide all humans into four blood groups. These are group A (A antigen); group B (B antigen); group AB (both antigens); and group O (neither antigen). Of course, what group you are does not affect the way you look. But it is important when donating (giving) blood, or when receiving blood from another person, after losing blood in an accident, for example. The blood group of the donor and the recipient must be the same, or there can be severe problems. The red blood cells of the person receiving the wrong blood may stick together and block blood vessels, killing the person the blood was meant to help.

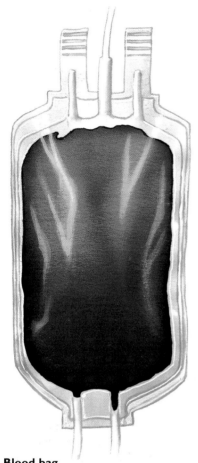

Blood bag
If someone donates (gives) blood, it is stored in a bag like this. The bag is sterile — free from germs. Inside is a chemical that stops the blood clotting and becoming solid.

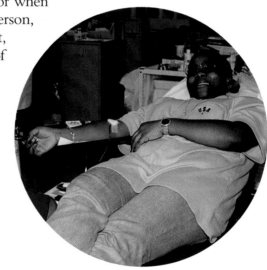

Blood donor
A blood donor is an adult who volunteers to give blood so that it can be used in hospitals. The amount of blood taken is less than 600 millilitres (1 pint). It does not take long for the body to make up the lost amount.

Blood bank
Just as money is stored in a bank, so is blood. Blood in a bank is identified by its group — A, B, AB or O — and kept until it is needed. If a person loses blood in an accident or during an operation, blood of the right group is taken from the bank to give to the patient. This is called a blood transfusion.

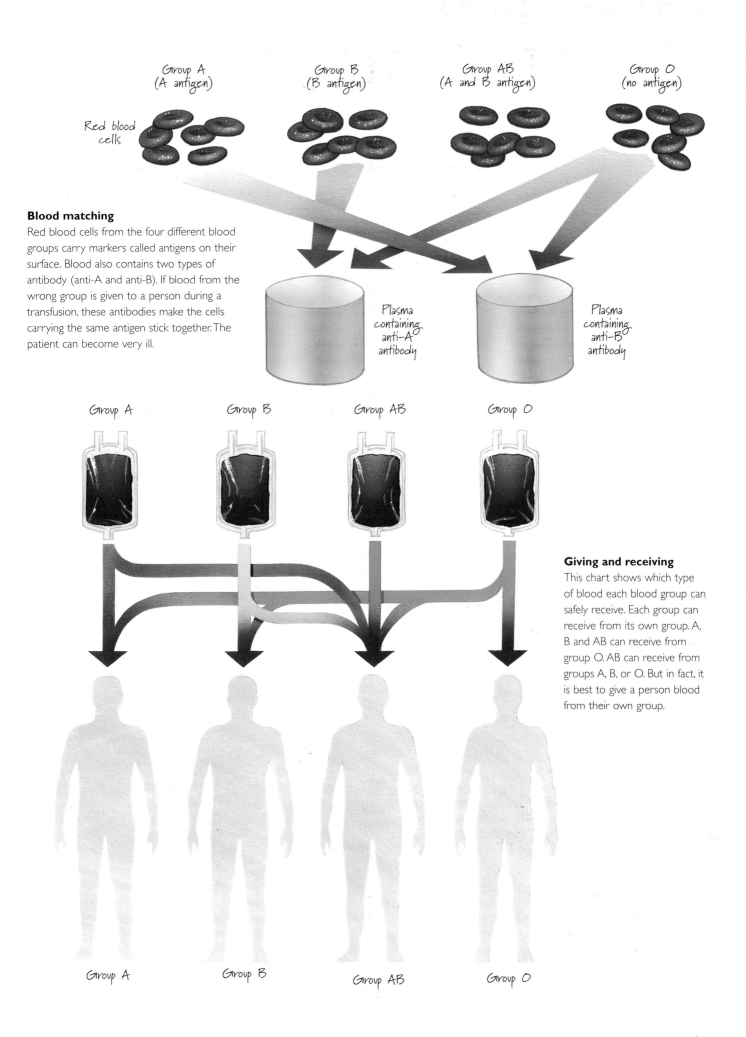

Group A
(A antigen)

Group B
(B antigen)

Group AB
(A and B antigen)

Group O
(no antigen)

Red blood
cells

Blood matching

Red blood cells from the four different blood groups carry markers called antigens on their surface. Blood also contains two types of antibody (anti-A and anti-B). If blood from the wrong group is given to a person during a transfusion, these antibodies make the cells carrying the same antigen stick together. The patient can become very ill.

Plasma
containing
anti-A
antibody

Plasma
containing
anti-B
antibody

Group A

Group B

Group AB

Group O

Giving and receiving

This chart shows which type of blood each blood group can safely receive. Each group can receive from its own group. A, B and AB can receive from group O. AB can receive from groups A, B, or O. But in fact, it is best to give a person blood from their own group.

Group A

Group B

Group AB

Group O

FIRST AID

First aid kit
A first aid kit should contain all the things needed to provide 'first' and immediate aid for injuries, before a doctor or nurse arrives.

Accidents – even small ones – can often damage blood vessels and cause bleeding. It is important to know basic first aid so bleeding can be stopped.

Even if a wound is very small and bleeding stops of its own accord, the wound still needs to be cleaned to make sure that it is not infected with germs. Bruises occur if you fall or knock against something and cause an injury with bleeding under the skin. This produces a bluish colour at first, which gradually turns yellow and then disappears. Bruises can be very sore, but the pain can be relieved simply by applying an ice pack immediately after the injury.

Apart from cuts and bruises, another common problem affecting the circulatory system is fainting. When someone faints they lose consciousness for a short time. This is because not enough oxygen is reaching the brain, perhaps because they have been standing still for a long time or sometimes because of a sudden shock. The best way to treat someone who has fainted is to lie them down and raise their feet higher than their head, so that normal blood flow to the brain is restored.

Inside the kit
The kit should include bandages, sterile dressings, adhesive dressings, antiseptic cream, scissors, safety pins and tweezers.

Severe bleeding
It is important to stop severe bleeding. It may help to get the patient to lie down. Raise the affected part of the body above the patient's head to lessen the bleeding. Press on the wound with your fingers, or preferably a sterile dressing. Then bandage the dressing in place and seek help.

Minor wounds
Minor bleeding from a cut, graze or other wound is easily controlled. Wash the wound under running water to remove any dirt. Dry it gently with sterile gauze. Cover the wound with an adhesive dressing.

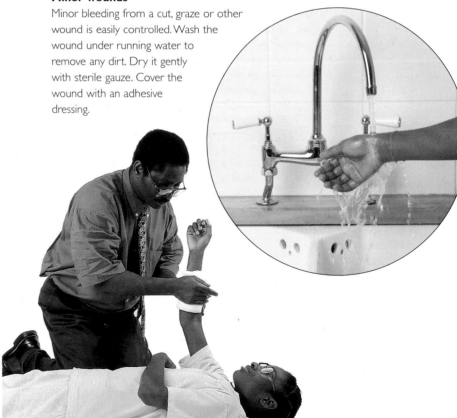

Fainting

Fainting happens when the brain does not receive enough oxygen because not enough blood is reaching it. If someone has fainted, make them comfortable. Raise their legs on a cushion to help blood to flow to the brain. Reassure the casualty that everything is all right as he or she regains consciousness. Make sure there is plenty of air in the room if you are indoors.

Bruises

Bruises are caused by bleeding inside the body. If possible, raise the affected part of the body. Apply a cold compress to help reduce blood flow. A cold compress is a pad soaked in cold water. This can be held in place with a bandage.

Nosebleed

Sometimes tiny blood vessels inside the nose break and blood pours out of the nostril. If this happens, sit down and lean forward. Pinch the nose just where the hard bit meets the softer bit. Keep pinching for 10 minutes, then release your fingers. If the nosebleed continues, pinch again until the bleeding stops.

Icepack

You can use an icepack to cool down a bruise. This can be made by wrapping ice cubes in a cloth. Hold the pack against the injury for about 20 minutes to cool it down.

CIRCULATORY DISEASES

Swollen artery

This is a special X-ray – an angiogram – of the arteries leaving the heart. One of them has a balloon-like swelling in it. This has happened because the artery wall is thinner than it should be. In fact, the wall is so thin it may burst.

Like any other body system, the circulatory system can go wrong. Problems are often caused by the blood vessels – the blood's delivery system – becoming blocked and stopping the flow.

In a disease called atherosclerosis, layers of fatty material build up inside arteries. Gradually the artery gets narrower and narrower. When it is very narrow a blood clot may form and block it completely. If this happens the blood supply to a particular organ is cut off.

If the blockage takes place in arteries supplying the brain it can cause a stroke. If its blood supply is cut off, that part of the brain soon dies. The person affected can no longer move the part of their body that is controlled by that part of the brain.

If a blockage occurs in a coronary artery supplying the heart it can cause a heart attack. Part of the heart's muscle dies, so that the heart works less efficiently. A heart attack can make a person very ill, and will kill them if the whole heart stops working.

Atherosclerosis is often linked to lifestyle. People who smoke, eat fatty food, and take little exercise are much more likely to suffer from it.

Clotting

This shows a clot forming inside a blood vessel as a result of a circulatory disease. The disease has made the inside of the artery rough, and the rough surface has encouraged the clot to form. This abnormal sort of clot – called a thrombus – can cause heart attacks or strokes.

Heart attack

The coronary arteries supply heart muscle with food and oxygen. If these arteries become narrower or blocked by a build-up of fatty material, the muscle in part of the heart may be cut off from its blood supply. If this happens, that part of the heart dies, and the person has a heart attack. In some cases, the heart attack kills the person.

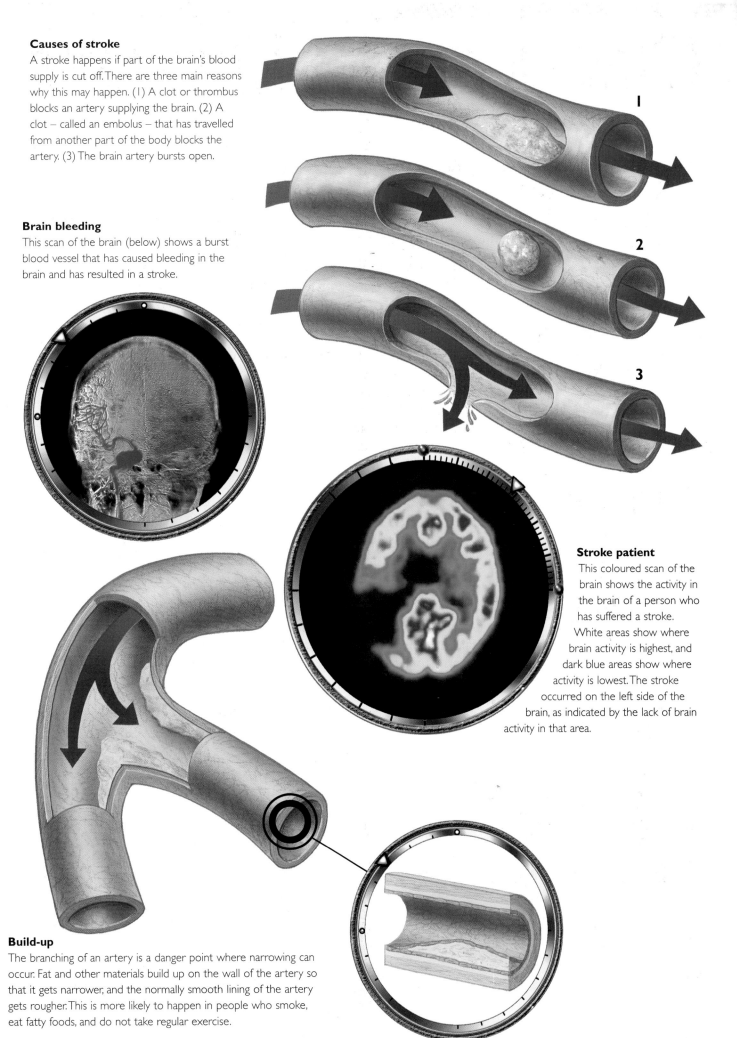

Causes of stroke

A stroke happens if part of the brain's blood supply is cut off. There are three main reasons why this may happen. (1) A clot or thrombus blocks an artery supplying the brain. (2) A clot – called an embolus – that has travelled from another part of the body blocks the artery. (3) The brain artery bursts open.

1

2

3

Brain bleeding

This scan of the brain (below) shows a burst blood vessel that has caused bleeding in the brain and has resulted in a stroke.

Stroke patient

This coloured scan of the brain shows the activity in the brain of a person who has suffered a stroke. White areas show where brain activity is highest, and dark blue areas show where activity is lowest. The stroke occurred on the left side of the brain, as indicated by the lack of brain activity in that area.

Build-up

The branching of an artery is a danger point where narrowing can occur. Fat and other materials build up on the wall of the artery so that it gets narrower, and the normally smooth lining of the artery gets rougher. This is more likely to happen in people who smoke, eat fatty foods, and do not take regular exercise.

GLOSSARY

ANTIBODY
A chemical that helps defend the body against germs by destroying them. Antibodies are released by lymphocytes.

ANTIGEN
A chemical that is found on the surface of germs such as bacteria. Antigens cause the release of antibodies.

AORTA
The largest artery in the body and the main artery through which blood leaves the heart. The aorta has branches that travel to all parts of the body.

ARTERIOLE
Narrow blood vessel that is the smallest branch of an artery. Arterioles branch to form even smaller capillaries.

ARTERY
A blood vessel that carries blood away from the heart. Arteries have thick walls to withstand the high pressure produced when the heart beats.

ATRIUM
The upper chamber found on each side of the heart. Blood enters the heart through the left and right atria.

CAPILLARY
The smallest type of blood vessel. Capillaries are very narrow and they carry blood through the body's tissues, supplying individual cells with what they need.

CELL
The smallest living unit in the human body. There are billions of cells in the body. Different types of cells – such as blood cells – have different jobs to do.

CORONARY ARTERY
Artery that supplies the muscular wall of the heart with blood. There are two coronary arteries that carry oxygen and food to right and left sides of the heart.

DIASTOLE
One stage in the heartbeat cycle. During diastole, the heart relaxes and the atria fill with blood from the body and lungs.

HAEMOGLOBIN
Orange-red coloured substance found in red blood cells. Haemoglobin picks up oxygen in the lungs and releases it where it is needed.

HEART
Muscular pump that pushes blood around the body. The heart automatically contracts about once a second to pump blood along the blood vessels.

IMMUNIZATION
The act of making someone immune - or protected from - a particular disease. During immunization a vaccine is injected into the body. This helps the body's immune system fight infection.

LYMPH NODE
Swelling found at intervals along a lymph vessel. Lymph nodes filter lymph as it passes through them, and destroy any germs it is carrying.

LYMPHOCYTE
Type of white blood cell found in blood and the lymphatic system that helps defend the body. Lymphocytes produce antibodies, chemicals that destroy invading germs.

MACROPHAGE
Type of white blood cell found wandering in tissues and in the lymphatic system. Macrophages help defend the body by eating and digesting germs.

MONOCYTE
Type of white blood cell. Monocytes protect the body by eating and digesting germs. Some become larger and fiercer macrophages during an infection.

NEUTROPHIL
Type of white blood cell. Neutrophils help defend the body by squeezing out through capillary walls to eat germs in the tissues.

PATHOGEN
The correct name for a germ. Pathogens - such as bacteria or viruses - can invade the body and cause disease. Blood cells fight the body's infection by pathogens.

PLASMA
The liquid, watery part of blood. Plasma is a yellowish liquid in which red blood cells, white blood cells, and platelets are suspended.

PLATELET
A cell fragment found in the blood. Platelets play a vital role in blood clotting. Clotting ensures that the body does not lose too much blood if a blood vessel is damaged.

RED BLOOD CELL
The most numerous type of cell carried by the blood. Red blood cells carry oxygen. They are packed with an orange-red substance called haemoglobin.

SEMILUNAR VALVE
Valve found in the heart at the point where blood leaves each ventricle. Semilunar valves stop blood flowing back into the heart when the heart relaxes.

SYSTOLE
Contraction of part of the heart. During atrial systole the atria contract to push blood into the ventricles. During ventricular systole, the ventricles contract to push blood around the body.

VEIN
A blood vessel that carries blood towards the heart. Veins have thinner walls than arteries, and have valves to stop blood flowing backwards away from the heart.

VENA CAVA
The largest vein in the body. The superior (upper) vena cava collects blood from the upper part of the body, and the inferior (lower) vena cava from the lower part. Both open into the right atrium of the heart.

VENULE
Smallest branch of a vein formed by capillaries joining together. Venules join up to form veins.

WHITE BLOOD CELL
Cells found in the blood that are colourless. White blood cells are less numerous than red. They enable the body to fight infection.

INDEX

Acknowledgements

The publishers wish to thank the following for supplying photographs for this book: Robert Becker/Custom Medical Stock Photo/Science Photo Library (SPL) 31 (BR); Biology Media/SPL 36 (BL); Biophoto Associates/SPL 21 (T); Prof. S Cinti, Universite d'Ancone, CNRI/SPL 3, 11 (TR); CNRI/SPL back cover (BL), 6 (TL, CL, BL), 7, 8 (BR), 24 (B), 25; A B Dowsett/SPL 26 (BL); Eye of Science/SPL 44 (CR); GCa-CNRI/SPL 12 (CR); Jan Hinsch/SPL 30 (TR); Karen Knight/National Blood Service 40 (CR); Bill Longcore/SPL 21 (BR); Dr P Marazzi/SPL 33 (T); Jerry Mason/SPL 40 (BL); Matt Meadows/Peter Arnold Inc./SPL 19 (TL); Miles Kelly Archives 4 (TR); Prof. P M Motta/Dept of Anatomy, University 'La Sapienza', Rome/SPL 31 (TR); Prof. P M Motta and Prof. G Macchiarelli/SPL front cover (TL), 4, 14 (BR), 15 (TR); NIBSC/SPL 27 (TR); Philippe Plailly/SPL front cover (CR), 13 (BR); D Phillips/SPL 26 (TR), 36 (TL); SPL 19 (B), 22 (TL), 23 (CL), 28 (BR), 29 (TR, C), 38 (BR), 44 (TL), 45 (CL, CR); Secchi, Lecaque, Roussel, UCLAF–CNRI/SPL 9 (CL), 33 (B), 35 (B); Pat Spillane 18, 42 (TL, TC; BR, models Dr Joseph Akinwumi and Gbemisola Akinwumi; CR), 43 (T, model Africa Green; C, B, models Dr Joseph Akinwumi and Gbemisola Akinwumi).

The publishers also wish to thank Boots the Chemist Plc and the National Blood Service for their help.